Wendell Berry

Confluence American Authors Series
James R. Hepworth, Series Editor
Lewis-Clark State College

TCAAS4

AMERICAN AUTHORS SERIES

Wendell Berry

edited by

Paul Merchant

Confluence Press, Inc.   Lewiston, Idaho

Library of Congress Catalogue Number 91-73134
ISBN: 0-917652-89-4 (cloth) / 0-917652-88-6 (paper)

Publication of this book is made possible by grants from The Idaho Commission on the Arts, a state agency, and the National Endowment for the Arts in
Washington, D.C., a federal agency.

Published by
Confluence Press, Inc.
8th Avenue & 6th Street
Lewiston, Idaho 83501

Distributed to the trade by
National Book Network
4720-A Boston Way
Lanham, Maryland 20706

About the Series

The aim of this series is to present the best in contemporary critical opinion on modern and contemporary American authors alongside interviews, excerpts, bibliographies, letters, photographs, and manuscript selections. In some cases, as with Nancy Colberg's descriptive bibliography of Wallace Stegner, we limit volumes to a single task. Regardless, our purpose for publishing each volume remains essentially the same: to make a real and lasting contribution to American literary studies. We hope to focus attention on modern and contemporary American authors whose work merits close examination, but especially upon those writers, like Wendell Berry, whose work recognizes that in being American our literature is intimately connected with a place. And that *that* place is a story that has already happened many times and is continuing to happen.

"To have lost, wantonly, / the ancient forests, the vast grasslands," Wendell Berry writes, "is our madness, the presence / in our very bodies of our grief." Our sanity, therefore, may not only depend upon our power to restore and preserve the earth, to witness and recognize our limitations, to nurture and care for all that we have been given, but also to produce a fundamental change within our human natures. Certainly, such change is possible given the history of our recorded experiences. Lincoln's 1862 Emancipation Proclamation, for example, put an end to the barbaric curse of slavery upon our continent. While the skeptics continue to argue that there will always be war, the rest of us must put an end to it as well.

And that brings me back to the subject of Wendell Berry and the purpose of this series of books. After reading his work (and occasionally publishing some of it) and considering what both his detractors and his champions have had to say, I believe I am well within the bounds of reason to suggest that Wendell Berry has become a new *kind* of American writer: one whose life and work harmonize with each other in ways that are as radical now as they once were traditional. Like Jefferson's, Berry's versatility—as farmer, teacher, poet, essayist, as environmentalist and theorist— must pose a problem of considerable dimensions for those who proclaim the value and necessity of "specialization." As its editor, my own hope for this series is that each of its volumes reminds us that American literature embraces a wide range of forms that remain vital in the hands of master practitioners.

James R. Hepworth, Series Editor

Table of Contents

Acknowledgements

I am pleased to acknowledge considerable assistance from others in the making of this volume. The following kindly gave their permission to reprint, or to use quotations from, work first published under their imprint: Jack Shoemaker and North Point Press; Glenn Storhaug and Five Seasons Press; the Associated University Presses for Bucknell University Press; Duke University Press; and Sierra Club Books. The photographers and copyright holders of photographs included here, Tanya Berry, Dan Carraco, James Baker Hall, Guy Mendes,* Pam Spaulding, and Christopher Meatyard, were most cooperative in allowing use of the photographs, and in clarifying some of their dates and locations. The writers and scholars whom I approached for contributions not only responded generously, but in many cases directed me most helpfully toward other contributors.

Andrew J. Angyal of Enon College, North Carolina, currently himself preparing a volume in the Twayne series on Wendell Berry, offered salutary suggestions for the Bibliography, as did Russell Freedman, of Second Life Books, Lanesborough, Massachusetts, who is at work on a full descriptive

*Jonathan Greene and Gnomon Press

bibliography of editions of Wendell Berry's work. My thanks are also due to Pat Norton, for skillfully keyboarding a sometimes unruly manuscript. I have of course been much helped throughout by James Hepworth and his able staff at Confluence Press, whose enthusiasm for the project was a constant encouragement.

My greatest gratitude is due to Wendell and Tanya Berry, who provided unpublished material, took valuable time to scrutinize and improve the Chronology and Bibliography, and searched out the photographs. Their greatest generosity was in allowing me to believe that this book was not a further intrusion on their peace of mind. I am grateful to them for helping it forward so unreservedly.

Wendell Berry

Introduction

This volume is, to my knowledge, the first to be devoted to the work of Wendell Berry, the Kentucky farmer-poet, novelist, teacher, and essayist. That such a volume has not appeared earlier is worthy of comment. Wendell Berry has been well known as a poet and novelist since the 1960s, and the readership for his essays, already established in the Sixties, greatly expanded with the Sierra Club publication in 1977 of his trenchant *The Unsettling of America*. He has been an eloquent and influential voice, a flawless stylist and combative polemicist, for two and a half decades, and at least two generations of American writers, one coming of age in the Sixties, and the other, again ecologically conscious, now finding its voice, have acknowledged him as colleague and mentor. When inviting contributions to this volume I was struck by the universal warmth of the responses I received from those whom I approached. In their eagerness to participate I saw a true reflection of the community values that Berry has preached and practiced.

Yet Wendell Berry continues to maintain a generous arm's-length distance from the cultural establishment, despite his record as a distinguished academic and memorable voice in debates of national importance. The reasons for this distance are worth stating, for they do him honor. Without being in any way marginal, he has chosen to articulate the concerns and ideals of a region; having established himself in New York, he returned to Kentucky, in reverse of the familiar pattern. A vigorous opponent of specialization in modern industrial farming, he is himself a person of many dimensions, who resists simple classification. In a world of rapid turnover, immediate gratification and headlines, he is a traditionalist, taking the long view. He is not fashionable, because he has resisted the very tendencies in national life that contribute to fashion. He is distrustful of celebrity, and no doubt regards exploratory intrusions into the lives of "personalities" with the same distaste as he does the strip mining of land. Fearless in speaking out on public issues, he greatly values privacy. In all these ways, he presents academic and media critics with an animal difficult to capture, let alone tame. Most of all, he articulates his own positions with a clarity that makes exposition redundant.

Berry is also, disconcertingly for critics, a prolific author, and one who shows no signs of resting on his laurels. A quick count shows a current tally of twenty-five full-length texts, most of them in print. There has always been an admirable consistency among all areas of his work, and occasionally a most interesting interdependence between the genres—for example, the most recent novel, *Remembering*, which echoes the concerns of some of the essays, in places quite directly. Yet Berry is at any stage liable to surprise the reader who has him pigeonholed. This is most evident in the essay collections. The first, *The Long-Legged House* (1969), relates national, local, and personal moral questions—Vietnam, Kentucky strip mining, his own return to his childhood roots—showing from the start an ability to investigate analogies between issues of public and private morality. *The Hidden Wound* (1970) deals with racism, scrutinizing his own early memories in the light of a wider historical awareness. *The Unforeseen Wilderness* (1971) narrates a personal journey into Kentucky's Red River Gorge, in a series of meditations accompanied by the photographs of Eugene Meatyard: an elegiac and angry book about the planned destruction of a place of beauty. These three books, all quite different in subject-matter, share a motif: the duty of taking personal responsibility for current conditions and events. There is as much of Thoreau's civil disobedience in Berry as there is of the nature journal.

The following three collections of essays, *A Continuous Harmony* (1972), *The Unsettling of America* (1977), and *The Gift of Good Land* (1981), take on with vigor the task of analyzing the values and farming practices of contemporary America, and of proposing remedies for the ills found there. In all three volumes (indeed, in all three of their subtitles) Berry makes a specific connection between culture and agriculture. These are seen as mirrors of each other, and as interdependent on one another, so that successes and failures in one are lived out as consequences in the other. The key to both is education, which in Berry often means memory, the knowledge of how a thing is done properly. This double imperative, of land stewardship and the training of educated legislators, was from the start a motive force in Revolutionary America, as Berry makes clear at the opening of an essay in *The Unsettling of America*: "In the mind of Thomas Jefferson, farming, education, and democratic liberty were indissolubly linked."

The latest essay collections, *Standing by Words* (1983), *Home Economics* (1987), and *What Are People For?* (1990), continue with increasing sharpness and penetration to investigate the concerns of the earlier volumes. But now a triple connection (latent from the beginning) is made explicit: that between farming, marriage, and poetry, three crafts requiring patience, an understanding of conditions, and an investment of time and energy in a future. Here the small community (the family, the local culture) and "the great community" (a phrase of Wallace Stegner's discussed in *What Are People For?*) share the same task, that of nourishing, in Stegner's words, "in solitude, in quiet, and in the company of the past, the great community of human experience." This dual task of memory and human responsibility is expressed in the title of the latest novel, *Remembering* (1988), and is the subject of the short story "*Are You All Right?* ", first printed here. It is equally a major theme in the previous novels, *Nathan Coulter* (1960), *A Place on Earth* (1967), and *The Memory of Old Jack* (1974), all of them set in the Kentucky community that Berry calls Port William, and in the short story collection *The Wild Birds: Six Stories of the Port William Membership* (1986).

In the two prose forms of essay and fiction, the treatment of themes shows a gradual organic development, whereby themes and concepts ("tradition," "memory," "marriage," "culture") recur in new contexts, with their meanings enhanced, or as metaphors linking two ideas for the first time. This process of defining terms, freshening and clarifying them, showing both their root significance and their metaphoric potential, is basic to Berry's craft, and may perhaps also be a stimulus to his imagination. It is much like the restoration of land, the revitalization of an overworked resource. A number of essays in this book give examples of such definitions and redefinitions at work. The process is at its most delicate and refined in Berry's poetry, gathered in nine individual volumes in addition to the *Collected Poems* of 1985. The poems, mostly terse but fully argued meditations, are Berry's most effective antidote to the forces of depersonalization, and perform the rituals of remembering—love, locality, the presence of the numinous—in their most focused form.

Part of "the work of local culture" (as expressed in an essay of that title in *What Are People For?*) is the telling and retelling of stories, for entertainment, for instruction, and for the preservation of history. Berry notes that children were always present on these occasions, called locally "sitting till bedtime." His description makes it clear that the entertainment industry has supplanted the art of story-telling, even where it was strongest and most valued, and Berry's urgent determination to tell the stories of his own community, preserving its local idioms, is quite literally the defense of a culture, as important as the preservation of a minority language in the survival of a national identity. The act of memory preserves a valued way of life, exactly as the maintenance of a deep and healthy topsoil preserves the fertility of the land—Berry makes the analogy explicit in the vivid opening paragraphs of this same essay.

The act of remembering is also, in oral poetry and song, probably the earliest way found by humans to record what was distinctive and valuable, and the successors of those first poets, the tellers of epics, may well have provided each of their cultures with crucial definitions of history. In the absence of oral epics, it is hard to imagine histories that would be more than current calendars of events; the epics gave such calendars depth and perspective. It is, I think, in this spirit that Berry's work so naturally refers to the narrative tradition that includes the makers of epic: *The Odyssey, Huckleberry Finn* and *Anna Karenina* in *The Hidden Wound*; the Homeric reaping in *The Wild Birds*; the Bible and Milton throughout his work; and more overtly, in *Standing by Words*, Homer, Dante, Spenser, Wordsworth, Pound. In the work of Wendell Berry, speech both preserves local tradition and keeps intact the continuous chain of poetry. This is one way to redefine in our time an ancestral *pietas*.

Perhaps it is in the same spirit that a number of contributors to this volume, when asked to write on Berry, chose to tell stories about him. These stories are of wide variety. We catch him in fragmentary glimpses: crouched to smell the odor of fox in a woodchuck hole in Kentucky; speaking in honor of Edward Abbey in the wilderness of Utah; or remarking on a potter's training in Japan. These vignettes, these tiny narratives, in their range of place and activity, form themselves into a body of commentary. They indicate an openness to experience, a belonging to the wider world as much as to the local. In telling their stories about him, his friends and colleagues show the reach of his concerns. Stories and fables are as analytical as essays, and often last longer in the mind. Where Berry's Andy Catlett tells the story of a remembered flood, in the first piece in this volume, we are glad to listen to a narrative that, for all its truth to an actual occurrence, has echoes of more ancient deluges. We are reminded how those who lived before the Flood survived in the oral narratives.

In the face of Berry's collected work, where he has written with such clarity, and so definitively, about those aspects of the world that he finds important, what is the responsibility of such a volume as this? It presents unpublished work by the author—in this case an original story and a sequence of new poems, *Sabbaths 1988*. And it can let the author speak for himself directly, as he does here in the reprint of his interview "A Question a Day." Such a volume can also provide a forum for critics to focus attention on traditions where the work takes its place—the epic, or agrarian writing, or didactic poetry—when the author has left such commentary to others. Most of the essays collected here, three of which are reprinted and the remainder written specially for the occasion, are of this kind. And this volume allows a select handful of Berry's associates to speak of him more personally. These formal criticisms and personal reminiscences should be seen together as a testimony to the neighborliness of Wendell Berry, his responsiveness to the community, small and great, his putting into practice of his ideas. It is in this neighborliness, throughout his many commitments as practical farmer, conservationist, teacher, writer, member of a family and of a community, that Wendell Berry shows us (with characteristic lightness of touch, humor, and lack of pretension) how to approach the task of being a responsible citizen.

Paul Merchant

Chronology

1934   born Wendell Erdman Berry, native of Henry County, Kentucky, on 5 August

1956   receives A.B. from University of Kentucky

1957   marries Tanya Amyx on 29 May; their children will be Mary Dee Berry (now Smith) and Pryor Clifford Berry. Receives M.A. from University of Kentucky

1958-59   Wallace Stegner Writing Fellowship, Stanford University

1959-60   teaches in Department of English, Stanford University

1960   *Nathan Coulter*, novel

1961-62   in Europe on Guggenheim Fellowship

1962   awarded Vachel Lindsay Prize by *Poetry*

1962-64   member of English faculty and director of first-year English program, New York University

1964   *November twenty six, nineteen sixty three*, poem, and *The Broken Ground*, poems. Joins English faculty, University of Kentucky at Lexington

1965   moves to Lanes Landing Farm, Port Royal, Kentucky; has farmed this land, adding to it and improving it, continuously since 1965. Receives Rockefeller Fellowship

1967   awarded Bess Hokin Prize by *Poetry. A Place on Earth*, novel

1968   *Openings*, poems; *The Rise*, non-fiction

1969   wins Borestone Mountain Poetry Awards. *The Long-Legged House*, non-fiction

1970   *Farming: A Hand Book*, poems; *The Hidden Wound*, non-fiction

1971   elected Distinguished Professor of English, University of Kentucky. Receives National Institute of Arts and Letters Literary Award. *The Unforeseen Wilderness*, non-fiction, with photographs by Gene Meatyard

1972   *A Continuous Harmony*, essays

1973   *The Country of Marriage*, poems. Appointed Professor of English, University of Kentucky

1974   wins Emily Balch Prize, *The Virginia Quarterly. The Memory of Old Jack*, novel

1975   first place award from Friends of American Writers for *The Memory of Old Jack*

1976   receives honorary doctorate from Centre College

1977   *Clearing*, poems; *The Unsettling of America*, essays. Resigns from faculty of University of Kentucky

1977-81   contributing editor, Rodale Press (*New Farm; Organic Gardening and Farming*)

1980   *A Part*, poems

1981   *The Gift of Good Land*, essays. *Recollected Essays 1965-80*. Receives honorary doctorate from Transylvania College

1982   *The Wheel*, poems

1983   *Standing by Words*, essays. Receives honorary doctorate from Berea College

1984   editor, with Wes Jackson and Bruce Colman, of *Meeting the Expectations of the Land*, essays

1985   *Collected Poems 1957-1982*

1986   *The Wild Birds*, stories. Receives honorary doctorate from University of Kentucky

1987   returns to teaching at University of Kentucky. *Home Economics*, essays; *Sabbaths*, poems. Jean Stein Award, American Academy of Arts and Letters. Receives honorary doctorate from Santa Clara University

1988   *Remembering*, novel; *Traveling at Home*, poems and prose. Receives honorary doctorate from Eureka College

1989   Lannan Foundation Award for non-fiction

1990   *What Are People For?*, essays; *Harlan Hubbard: Life and Work*, criti-
            cism.

New Works
by
Wendell Berry

Are You All Right?

Wendell Berry

The spring work had started, and I needed a long night's rest, or that was my opinion, and I was about to go to bed, but then the telephone rang. It was Elton. He had been getting ready for bed too, I think, and it had occurred to him then that he was worried.

"Andy, when did you see the Rowanberrys?"

I knew what he had on his mind. The river was in flood. The backwater was over the bottoms, and Art and Mart would not be able to get out except by boat or on foot.

"Not since the river came up."

"Well, neither have I. And their phone's out. Mary, when did Mart call up here?"

I heard Mary telling him, "Monday night," and then, "It was Monday night," Elton said to me. "I've tried to call every day since, and I can't get anybody. That's four days."

"Well, surely they're all right."

"Well, that's what Mary and I have been saying. Surely they are. They've been taking care of themselves a long time. But, then, you never know."

"The thing is, we *don't* know."

We knew what we were doing, and both of us were a little embarrassed about it. The Rowanberry Place had carried that name since the first deeds were recorded in the log cabin that was the first courthouse at Hargrave. Rowanberrys had been taking care of themselves there for the better part of two hundred years. We knew that Arthur and Martin Rowanberry required as little worrying about as anybody alive. But now, in venturing to worry about them, we had put them, so to speak, under the sign of mortality. They were, after all, the last of the Rowanberrys, and they were getting old. We were uneasy in being divided from them by the risen water and out of touch. It caused us to think of things that could happen.

Elton said, "It's not hard, you know, to think of things that could happen."

"Well," I said, "do you think we'd better go see about them?"

He laughed. "Well, we've thought, haven't we? I guess we'd better go."

"All right. I'll meet you at the mailbox."

I hung up and went to get my cap and jacket.

"Nobody's heard from Art and Mart for four days," I said to Flora. "Their phone's out."

"And you and Elton are going to see about them," Flora said. She had been eavesdropping.

"I guess we are."

Flora was inclined to be amused at the way Elton and I imagined the worst. She did not imagine the worst. She just dealt with mortality as it happened.

I picked up a flashlight as I went out the door, but it was not much needed. The moon was big, bright enough to put out most of the stars. I walked out to the mailbox, and made myself comfortable, leaning against it. Elton and I had obliged ourselves to worry about the Rowanberrys, but I was glad all the same for the excuse to be out. The night was still, the country all silvery with moonlight, inlaid with bottomless shadows, and the air shimmered with the trilling of peepers from every stream and pond margin for miles, one full-throated sound filling the ears so that it seemed impossible that you could hear anything else.

And yet I heard Elton's pickup while it was still back on the ridge, and then light glowed in the air where the road starts down the hill, and then I could see his headlights. He turned into the lane and stopped and pushed the door open for me. I made room for myself among a bundle of empty feed sacks, two buckets, and a chain saw. We started back up the hill.

"Fine night," he said. He had lit a cigarette, and the cab was fragrant with smoke.

"It couldn't be better, could it?"

"Well, the moon could be just a little brighter, and it could be a teensy bit warmer."

I could hear that he was grinning. He was in one of his companionable moods, making fun of himself.

I laughed, and we rode without talking up out of the Katy's Branch valley and turned onto the state road.

"It's awful the things that can get into your mind," Elton said. "I'd hate it if anything was to happen to them."

The Rowanberrys were Elton's friends, and because they were his they were mine. Elton had known them ever since he was just a little half-orphan boy, living with his mother and older brothers on the next farm up the creek. He had got a lot of his raising by being underfoot and in the way at the Rowanberrys'. And in the time of his manhood the Rowanberry Place had been one of his resting places.

Elton worked hard and worried hard, and he was often in need of rest. But he had a restless mind, which meant that he could not rest on his own place in the presence of his own work. If he rested there, first he would begin to think about what he had to do, and then he would begin to do it.

To rest, he needed to be in somebody else's place. We spent a lot of Sunday afternoons down at the Rowanberrys', on the porch looking out into the little valley in the summertime, inside by the stove if it was winter. Art and Mart batched there together after their mother died, and, in spite of the electric lights and telephone and a few machines, they lived a life that would have been recognizable to Elias Rowanberry, who had marked his X in the county's first deed-book—a life that involved hunting and fishing and foraging as conventionally as it involved farming. They practiced an old-fashioned independence, an old-fashioned generosity, and an old-fashioned fidelity to their word and their friends. And they were hound men of the old correct school. They would not let a dog tree anywhere in ear-shot, day or night, workday or Sunday, without going to him. "It can be a nuisance," Art said, "but it don't hardly seem right to disappoint 'em."

Mart was the one Elton liked best to work with. Mart was not only a fine hand, but had a gift for accommodating himself to the rhythms and ways of his partner. "He can think your thoughts," Elton said. Between the two of them was a sympathy of body and mind that they had worked out and that they trusted with an unshaken, unspoken trust. And so Elton was always at ease and quiet in Mart's company when they were at rest.

Art was the rememberer. He knew what he knew and what had been known by a lot of dead kinfolks and neighbors. They lived on in his mind and spoke there, reminding him and us of things that needed to be remembered. Art had a compound mind as a daisy has a compound flower, and his mind had something of the unwary comeliness of a daisy. Something that happened would remind him of something that he remembered, which would remind him of something that his grandfather remembered. It was not that he "lived in his mind." He lived in the place, but the place was where the memories were, and he walked among them, tracing them out over the living ground. That was why we loved him.

We followed the state road along the ridges toward Port William, and then at the edge of town turned down the Willow Run Road. We went down the hill through the woods, and as we came near the floor of the valley Elton went more carefully and we began to watch. We crossed a little board culvert that rattled under the wheels, eased around a bend, and there was the backwater, the headlights glancing off it into the treetops, the road disappearing into it.

Elton stopped the truck. He turned off his headlights and the engine, and the quietness of the moonlight and the woods came down around us. I could hear the peepers again. It was wonderful what the road going under the water did to that place. It was not only that we could not go where we were used to going; it was as if a thought that we were used to thinking could not be thought.

"Listen!" Elton said. He had heard a barred owl off in the woods. He quietly rolled the window down.

And then, right overhead, an owl answered: "HOOOOOAWWW!"

And the far one said, "Hoo hoo hoohooaw!"

"Listen!" Elton said again. He was whispering.

The owls went through their whole repertory of hoots and clucks and cackles and gobbles.

"Listen to them!" Elton said. "They've got a lot on their minds." Being in the woods at night excited him. He was a hunter. And we were excited by the flood's interruption of the road. The rising of the wild water had moved us back in time.

Elton quietly opened his door and got out, and then, instead of slamming the door, just pushed it to. I did the same, and came around and followed him as he walked slowly down the road, looking for a place to climb out of the cut.

Once we had climbed the bank and stepped over the fence and were walking among the big trees, we seemed already miles from the truck. The water gleamed over the bottomlands below us on our right; you could not see that there ever had been a road in that place. I followed Elton along the slope through the trees. Neither of us thought to use a flashlight, though we each had one, nor did we talk. The moon gave plenty of light. We could see everything — the blooms of twinleaf, bloodroot, rue anemone, the little stars of spring beauties underfoot, and overhead the littlest branches, even the blooms on the sugar maples. The ground was soft from the rain, and we hardly made a sound. The flowers around us seemed to float in the shadows so that we walked like waders among stars, uncertain how far down to put our feet. And over the broad shine of the backwater the calling of the peepers rose like another flood, higher than the water flood, and thrilled and trembled in the air.

It was a long walk because we had to go around the inlets of the backwater that lay in every swag and hollow. Way off, now and again, we could hear the owls. Once we startled a deer, and stood still to listen while it plunged away into the shadows. And always we were walking among flowers. I wanted to keep thinking that they were like stars, but after a while I could not think so. They were not like stars. They did not have that hard, distant glitter. And yet in their pale, peaceful way, they shone. They collected their little share of light and gave it back. Now and then, when we came to an especially thick patch of them, Elton would point. Or he would raise his hand and we would stop a minute and listen to the owls.

I was wider awake than I had been all day. I would have been glad to go on walking all night long. Around us we could feel the year coming, as strong and wide and irresistible as a wind.

But we were thinking too of the Rowanberrys. That we were in a mood to loiter and did not loiter would have reminded us of them, if we had needed reminding. To go to their house, with the water up, would have required a long walk from any place we could have started. We were taking the shortest way, which left us with the problem that it was going to be a little too short. The best we could do, this way, would be to come down the valley until we would be across from the house but still divided from it by maybe half a mile of backwater. We could call to them from there. But what if we got no answer? What if the answer was trouble? Well, they had a boat over there. If they needed us, one of them could set us over in the boat. But what if we got no answer? What if, to put the best construction upon silence, they could not hear us? Well, we could only go as near as we could get, and call.

So if our walk had the feeling of a ramble, it was not one. We were going as straight to the Rowanberrys' house as the water and the lay of the land would allow. After a while we began to expect to see a light. And then we began to wonder if there was a light to see.

Elton stopped. "I thought we'd have seen their light by now."

I said, "They're probably asleep."

Those were the first words we had spoken since we left the truck. After so long, in so much quiet, our voices sounded small.

Elton went on among the trees and the shadows, and I followed him. We climbed over a little shoulder of the slope then, and saw one window shining. It was the light of an oil lamp, so their electricity was out too.

"And now we're found," Elton said. He sang it, just that much of the old hymn, almost in a whisper.

We went through a little more of the woods and climbed the fence into the Rowanberrys' hill pasture. We could see their big barn standing up black now against the moonlight on the other side of the road, which was on high ground at that place, clear of the backwater.

When were on the gravel we could hear our steps. We walked side by side, Elton in one wheeltrack, I in the other, until the road went under the water again. We were as close to the house then as we could get without a boat. We stopped and considered the distance.

And then Elton cupped his his hands around his mouth, and called: "Ohhhhh, Mart! Ohhhhh, Art!"

We waited, it seemed, while Art had time to say, "Did you hear somebody?" and Mart to answer, "Well, I *thought* so." We saw light come to another window, as somebody picked up a lamp and opened the hall door. We heard the front door open. And then Art's voice came across the water: "Yeeeaaah?"

And Elton called back: "Are you aaalll riiight?"

I knew they were. I was relieved. They were all right, and we were free to go back through the woods home to sleep.

But I know now that it was neither of the Rowanberrys who was under the sign of mortality that night. It was Elton. Before another April came he would be in his grave on the hill at Port William. Old Art Rowanberry, who had held him on his lap, would survive him by a dozen years.

And now that both of them are dead, I love to think of them standing with the shining backwater between them, while Elton's voice goes out across the distance, is heard, answered, and the other voice travels back: "Yeeeaaah!"

Sabbaths 1988

Wendell Berry

I

Now I have reached the age
of judgment giving sorrow
that many men have come to,
the verdict of regret,
remembering the world
once better than it is,
my old walkways beneath
the vanished trees, and friends
lost now in loss of trust.

And I recall myself
more innocent than I am,
gone past coming back
in the history of flaw,
except Christ dead and risen
in my own flesh shall judge,
condemn, and then forgive.

II

It is the destruction of the world
in our own lives that drives us
half insane, and more than half.
To destroy that which we were given
in trust: how will we bear it?
It is our own bodies that we give
to be broken, our bodies
existing before and after us
in clod and cloud, worm and tree
that we, driving or driven, despise
in our haste to die, our country
spent in shiny cars speeding
to junk. To have lost, wantonly,
the ancient forests, the vast grasslands
is our madness, the presence
in our very bodies of our grief.

III

Another year has returned us
to the day of our marriage
thirty-one years ago. Many times
we have known, and again forgot
in our cruel separateness,
that making touch that feelingly
persuades us what we are:
one another's and many others',
brought together as by a music
of singing birds hidden among
the leaves, or the memory of
small flowers in the dark grass.
How strange to think of children
yet to come, into whose making we
will be made, who will not know us
even so little as we know
ourselves, who have already gone
so far beyond our own recall.

IV

The world of machines is running
Beyond the world of trees
Where only a leaf is turning
In a small high breeze.

V

Always in the distance
the sound of cars is passing
on the road, that simplest form
going only two ways,
both ways away. And I
have been there in that going.

But now I rest and am
apart, a part of the form
of the woods always arriving
from all directions home,
this cell of wild sound,
the hush of the trees, singers
hidden among the leaves—

a form whose history is old,
needful, unknown, and bright
as the history of the stars
that tremble in the sky at night
like leaves of a great tree.

An Interview

A Question a Day:
A Written Conversation
with Wendell Berry

Mindy Weinreb

WEINREB: You have written in forms as distinct from each other as novels, essays, and short lyric poems. If the choice were yours, where would you want a reader of your work to begin?

BERRY: I think it is important to understand that a writer never has this choice. A reader may begin anywhere, and that simply means that every work should stand on its own legs. That said, I'm not sure that I would want the choice if I had it. My interest in my work is necessarily different from that of any reader. I am most interested in what I am doing and what I would like to do, whereas a reader can only be interested in what I have done.

WEINREB: Even though a writer cannot decide where a reader begins, he might have preferences or favorites from work already completed. What, for example, are the two or three poems that you would like to be known or remembered by?

BERRY: I have never tried to think in this way about my work, or anybody else's, because it doesn't interest me. One needs to know, or to try to know, which poems are good and which are not, of course, and one needs to make comparisons. But win, place, and show are not meaningful poetic categories to me. A poet would be fortunate, obviously, to be remembered past his or her lifetime by two or three poems, or even by one. But I am not satisfied by the idea that a poet's lifetime of work exists for two or three "best" or "near-perfect" or "unforgettable" poems to be put into some "golden treasury." I think that the lifetime of work has significance both in itself and in its service or disservice to the best possibilities of poetry and human culture, whether or not it is remembered. When I am doing my own work, so far as I can tell, I am not thinking at all about the possibility of being remembered or even of being read. I am trying to make a poem that I need to have made. I know that I don't need a bad poem. And so the issues for me, when it comes to issues, are what is done well and what is not, what coheres and what does not, what is true and what is not. I can't pretend that I can answer these questions unerringly, but these, nevertheless, are the questions that count. And for the worker they are the interesting questions.

WEINREB: It is, I think, misleading to suggest that we do not make value judgments about our creations, no matter how humble they may be. You don't want to compete, especially with yourself, and that I understand. But is there nothing that you care to talk about as standing more firmly on its own legs than other things that you have written?

BERRY: I didn't mean that I don't make judgments of my work, or that I don't try always to do better, but only that I don't try to rank my poems first, second, third, et cetera. That is appropriate in a livestock show, but it seems to me to have nothing much to do with poetry. I really doubt that it is important to know which is the number-one best poem of Yeats or Herbert. And I know I'm not interested in deciding which is my own best poem. The reason is simply that such judgments are extremely contestable. At any given time I have in mind several of my own poems that for one reason or another seem to stand out, but I would never name these publicly—partly for the reasons already given, and partly because I don't think it is a poet's business to make public judgments of his or her own work. What I always hope to do in my work is to make the forms more comprehensive, the connections plainer and stronger, the rhythms cleaner and more forceful and more coherent, the music clearer and finer. And of course when one's wish really is to do better, then one is not going to be stuck in admiration of what one has already done.

WEINREB: Will you mention some of the human issues that concern you? For instance, a recurring metaphor in your writing is that of marriage for many different kinds of agreements—all to some degree sacred.

BERRY: Human reality, as I understand it, can be diagramed as a series of concentric circles or spheres: nature, human economy and culture, community, household, marriage, and family. There is complex interdependency among all of these spheres, and each one and its connections with the others must be preserved. They must be kept together in some kind of union—consciously understood (though understanding can never be complete), loved, honored, and cherished—for which marriage, I suppose, is as good a metaphor as any. One of the uses of poetry is to keep this union alive in the minds of human beings, to whom its care and preservation have been entrusted.

WEINREB: Words like "care," "preservation," and "entrusted" suggest how much responsibility is invested in the act of writing poetry. And, like Williams, you seem to be consciously trying to bring the original meanings back to these words. Yet we live in a culture where what you call "immediate remedy" is promised to us by our language. Is the public's impatience with poetry the result of that?

BERRY: Williams said that men die miserably every day for lack of what is to be found in poetry. I too believe this. But not of all poetry. Not all poets put into their poems anything that can save or console. Poets decide by their poems how seriously they are willing to speak, how much of the community of living things they are willing to speak for or take responsibility for. And the practice of poetry in our time, as in times before, provides abundant means for avoiding this sort of seriousness. There are, for example, the well-known escapes into sensibility, estheticism, experiment-alism, closet autobiography, and a sort of academic industrialism. That, probably, is one reason for the public's impatience with poetry—or, more accurately, the public's indifference to it. Another reason is that poetry is not very seriously taught. The schools, for a long time, have had cold feet about the instructiveness of literature. Students aren't encouraged to read great works of literature for the sake of what they can learn from them —that is, about how to live their lives. We hear everywhere the emascula-ting phrase "as literature." We teach the Bible "as literature" on the quaint assumption that "as literature" it will have no power over us. We teach Dante and Shakespeare and Milton as literature, too—to deny their power to compel or challenge belief. We are fearful that some student may under-stand the parable of the prodigal son or *King Lear* as instructive about parenthood and sonship and daughterhood, as if anyone but a fool or a knave could help but read them so. Thus the public's astonishing assump-tion that poetry "doesn't have anything to do with anything" is simply what the public has been taught in schools and universities. I think that the idea that literature should instruct and delight is perfectly sound, provided we understand that it must do both at once.

WEINREB: Would you like to see young people receiving instruction from somewhere other than our schools, then, or are you asking that we recon-sider the kind of education we make available to the young through schools?

BERRY: If people were taught only in schools, they would never know much. And teaching is increasingly confined to schools. But what I meant by the previous answer was simply that literature should be taught as what it is: our memory, our delight, our faithful source of guidance and consolation. It is not a collection of laboratory specimens to be dissected or a lode of ruins and relics to be dug up and classified.

WEINREB: You have said that the written word has made our memories less reliable. Others have gone even further by remarking that printing has, tragically, made the elderly less essential to younger generations now that knowledge can be stored in books. As someone who relies on the written word but who also respects human traditions, you must have a reaction to that.

BERRY: It is not the written word that impairs memory, but dependence on the written word to the exclusion of the spoken. Some experience cannot be put wholly into writing. And so as dependence on writing grows, the communicated experience suffers a corresponding attenuation. The most complete speech is that of conversation in a settled community of some age, where what is said refers to and evokes things, people, places, and events that are commonly known. In such a community, to speak and hear is to remember. And this remembering can be aided, moreover, by mimicry, which is beyond the reach of writing. Thus it is possible for unwritten local tradition to preserve qualities of the voice and bearing and even the expressions and gestures of, say, a great-great-aunt past the time when those who knew her have died. It is not printing that has made the old inessential to the young—or that has made it possible for the young to think so. That has been caused by the dispersal of families and communities, and the consequent destruction of local cultures and economies. Local economy is the critical consideration here, for when the local economy is destroyed, then the young no longer *need* to hear what the old have to say; old memory loses its dignity in losing its worth, and thus the local speech, which is the vehicle—indeed, the very life and presence—of local memory, can be easily replaced by the necessarily cruder and remoter speech of television. It is this media speech, not literature, that replaces local speech and local memory.

WEINREB: You wrote about the importance of local economy in *The Gift of Good Land*. Do you honestly believe, however, that it's possible for us to return to systems like those the Amish or other small-scale farmers employ? And if not, what's going to happen?

BERRY: We can't "return" to anything, of course. We *can* see differences of quality and quantity and attempt to do what is best. The question, then, is not whether or not to go back to something left behind, but what is the proper scale, and the proper ratio of people to acres, in the use and care of the land. This question is urgent because, at the present scale and ratio, we are destroying both our land and our rural communities at a catastrophic rate. We have an abundance of examples, past and present, that suggest that small-scale agriculture is best for both land and people, and for an impressive variety of reasons. The large-scale agricultures that we know about, on the other hand, have proved destructive of land or people or both. The Amish are relevant to this issue simply because they are the group, in this country, that is farming best—that is, taking the best care of both land and people, and doing best economically. That they farm on a small scale, in terms both of technology and of land holdings, is one of the reasons for their success. If we don't take care of things, of course, we will be in want.

WEINREB: How are farming and poetry connected to each other in your mind? Also in *The Gift of Good Land*, you said that "a good farmer is a craftsman of the highest order, a kind of artist." Comment on this relationship, if you will.

BERRY: They are connected in my mind, to begin with, because I am a farmer and a poet—a poet who writes about farming, and a farmer who reads and thinks about poetry. But it is more complicated than that. I have come more and more to believe, with Eric Gill, that the only valid kind of distinction to be made between kinds of making is qualitative. Otherwise, human work is all art—all artifice or making-by-art. I do believe that "a *good* farmer is a craftsman of the highest order, a kind of artist." The finest farmers are masters of form. They must know how to do one thing while remaining mindful of many. They must bring many patterns into harmony. They must understand how diversity may be comprehended within unity. They must know how to deal with the unforeseen. And these are all characteristics of the finest poets. Also, there is a kinship among all arts or disciplines, and a knowledge of one imparts a sympathy for others and can be useful in learning another. I have farmed and been a student of farming most of my life, and I am sure that my understanding of farming has profoundly influenced my understanding of the art of writing and my work as a writer, though I suppose that would be hard to demonstrate.

WEINREB: You seem cautiously optimistic about the future of American farming. Are your feelings similar on the future of American poetry?

BERRY: I am hardly an optimist, but then I am hardly a predictor either. I am hopeful, because I know that some good work is being done in agriculture, in poetry, and in other essential disciplines. I am worried, because I wonder how successful a mere scattering of good workers can be in maintaining a continuity or a tradition. A strong tradition has to be broadly based, and we do not have a wide appreciation of good land use or good literature. Our public values, and our public schools, seem to be tending in the opposite direction.

WEINREB: Why, then, are you returning to the University of Kentucky to teach next fall after giving up on the universities once before?

BERRY: Well, maybe people who are worried about education ought to take part in it. But that I'm worried about education means that I'm worried about my participation in it. I quit teaching in 1977 with some very strong doubts about my ability to fit into university education as it had come to be, and the years since haven't relieved the doubts. I am a sort of agrarian traditionalist, and the universities are, pretty much without apology, in the service of the military-industrial state. My return to teaching should be regarded as experimental, I think.

WEINREB: What do you read for pleasure or instruction and, naturally, why?

BERRY: That is a hard question to answer because my reading has never been very systematic. I do a certain amount of reading about agriculture, but a lot of my "research" has consisted of things people have sent me in the mail. Sometimes I read in the hope of patching the holes in my education, but it is still full of holes. I read my friends. I read miscellaneous contemporary poetry in books and magazines. I return to Homer, Dante, Spenser, Shakespeare, Herbert, Milton, Marvell, Chaucer, Jonson, Pope, and others. Lately I have been reading John Clare, Henry Adams, Kathleen Raine, the Gospel of Matthew, Paul Johnson's *Modern Times*, Martin Lings's *The Secret of Shakespeare*, and am bogged down (for about the tenth time) in *The Pickwick Papers*. I read for instruction and pleasure, both at once.

WEINREB: On the matter of instruction, what is the difference between morality and amorality in literature to your mind?

BERRY: I suppose we have to allow the possibility that literature can be forthrightly or prescriptively moral—unless we want to deny any literary merit to, say, the Sermon on the Mount, which I don't think we can do. The problem here is that of authority: it takes a *lot* of authority for a moral prescription to rank as literature. If the prescription is merely personal or factional, then it seems to be not literature, but merely half an argument. To be moral, literature does not have to be prescriptively moral. But it does have to assume the obligation of honesty. I don't think it can fulfill this obligation perfectly, but it must attempt to do so. It must struggle ceaselessly against any impulse to falsify or reduce either the meanings of words or the values or the real complexities of subjects. I don't think that there is such a thing as a tenable amorality.

WEINREB: Okay, but is it possible for issues of religion or morality to permeate one's work to a point where they limit one's vision, rather than broadening and deepening it?

BERRY: A work of art is not a court or a penal system, and it had better not try to be. If a thing is fully imagined—as opposed to conceptualized or thought up—it will be just to the real complexity of experience. There does exist a highly oversimplified religious or moral mentality that condemns evil without, for instance, acknowledging its attractiveness or understanding the part it may play in a person's spiritual growth. Some people may go on as if sin were merely disgusting and something that "good people" do not do, but that has never been the way of the imagination. Dante did put a number of people into Hell, but the *Inferno* does not get its power from any superiority that he feels toward them. It is powerful because he knows all too well how they got there. The *Comedy* begins because he is in danger of ending up there himself, something he clearly understands.

WEINREB: Can a bad person be a good writer?

BERRY: Yes. It is possible for a bad person to write well. But I don't think that literary standards are the only ones that apply. This becomes clear if you consider that writing uses language, which is not a property merely of literature. In judging a literary work, it is legitimate, I would argue, to ask what its effect might be, or has been, on community life or on nature. Or to ask if it would be destructive of good values or tend to encourage unnecessary enmity or violence. I *don't*, however, think that such judgments should be made by a government. My fear is that if people don't make them, and make them intelligently, then sooner or later government *will* make them.

WEINREB: You have mentioned the Bible and made biblical allusions several times in your answers to my questions, and your writing elsewhere doesn't shy away from explicit references to Creation. How does religious belief figure into your judgments of literature?

BERRY: I don't see how religious belief can figure very directly in literary judgments. A Christian, for instance, who could not recognize the literary quality of good work by a Muslim or a Buddhist or an atheist would be a fool. But there is probably a valid religious issue that is coupled with the use and understanding of language, in literature and out. It would be very hard, it seems to me, to separate our language or our literary tradition from the biblical or Judeo-Christian tradition. This means, for one thing, that you can't make sense of Herbert or Milton or Eliot by reading or writing about them as if their belief was merely "subject matter." It means also that atheists should be very careful with words like "creative" or "creature." Our language, at its fullest and richest, is a language formed and informed by religious tradition and religious preoccupations. That is merely the fact of it. Something else that concerns me very much is that the effort to speak and write without religious reference produces a language that is severely impoverished and dull, and also serviceable to dangerous purposes. To use a language that concedes no creatureliness to plants and animals can abet an unduly proprietary attitude toward plants and animals. To use language that concedes no creatureliness or humanity to humans abets, sometimes, the most inhumane treatment of humans. To use language that does not acknowledge the existence of anything that cannot be measured implies a doom to the unmeasurable.

WEINREB: How is it possible to have so much faith in such a faithless time?

BERRY: This does not seem to me to be a faithless time. I think that people are, almost by definition, creatures of faith. Our time is not one of faithlessness, but one of misplaced faith. Atheism, after all, is a faith. You would have no trouble at all, now, in turning up people without religious faith who yet have faith in progress, in doctors, in the inevitable goodness of science or education, in the government, in the president, in the economy, et cetera, et cetera.

WEINREB: You are one of the few people I have met who actually lives what he believes in—or seems to.

BERRY: I guess you ought to say that I *try* to live what I believe in. Or when I'm at my best I do. The people I live with could tell you that my grades aren't all that good.

WEINREB: My guess is that you don't like to think in these terms, but do you adhere to the classical or the romantic notion of writing?

BERRY: I don't much trust those categories, or use them much in my thoughts. I certainly would not dismiss or ignore a body of work because of its category. Neither taste nor judgment, it seems to me, is categorical in nature, but particular and precise. For example, I love many poems by Wordsworth and Keats; I love Blake; and I also love many poems by Dryden, Pope, and Dr. Johnson. A categorizing mind, I guess, might find that confusing, but I ought to be able to account for my preferences, fairly exactly and responsibly, in terms of my taste and judgment. The terms "classic" and "romantic" are most useful to me in describing dangers or extremes to be avoided. There is a self-conscious or doctrinaire "classicism" that is too restrictive or exclusive, that leaves too much out or fails or refuses to consider everything that ought to be considered. That is dangerous. Equally dangerous is the extreme "romantic" individualism and the moral relativism that goes with it. That is the great monster-maker of our time: the manifest destiny of "self-realization." The world can always tolerate a few self-obsessed artists, I suppose. But people who can't fulfill themselves without dabbling in tyranny or in genetic or social or nuclear engineering are another matter.

WEINREB: I've never thought of the mad scientist as a romantic before. But that's a whole different matter, it seems to me. Let's talk more about your own work habits. Do you have any superstitions about or preconditions for work that you plan to do?

BERRY: "I didn't know there was but one idea about work—until it is done, it ain't done, and when it is done, it is": William Faulkner, "Shingles for the Lord."

WEINREB: That could just as easily be the farmer in you talking as the writer in you (or in Faulkner). As a man with a farm to run, how do you make time to write? Do you have a schedule for yourself as regular as the chores that must be done on your land?

BERRY: It's not all that extensive a farm, but it does require a lot of time and attention. I am usually able to write some all the year round. But from early spring until maybe sometime in October, whatever writing time I have is subject to interruption. In the late fall and in the winter it is more dependable; then I can do my early-morning chores and write until noon—except when I'm traveling too much, to lecture and read, which I do sometimes. In the afternoon, the year round, I like to work outdoors if the weather permits. I try to treat writing like any other kind of work. It is best, for me, when I can write every day, from breakfast until noon. That's about as long at a stretch as I can hope to write well. After that I need another job.

WEINREB: Regarding workmanship, do you revise much as you go along, or later, or not at all?

BERRY: I write in longhand, with a pencil, and make many changes and erasures as I go along. Every morning, before I begin, I read over and correct the work of the morning before. When I have finished a chapter or a story or essay, I read it aloud to Tanya, my wife, and make the corrections that this reading suggests to her and to me. Before she types it, I read it again and make further changes. Between typescript and publication many more changes may be made, according to suggestions made by Tanya, friends, editors, and myself. This usually continues after publication. All my copies of my own books have improvements in the margins. New editions of my books have always contained revisions. *A Place on Earth* was strenuously revised, mainly by cutting, and shortened by a third.

WEINREB: It puzzles me, then, that you say "a poem is not an object" in *Standing by Words*, because my impression has been, and you have reinforced it now, that all of your writing is carefully crafted.

BERRY: My way of revising poems is not quite so systematic, but it goes on as endlessly. By saying that a poem is not an object I meant that it is not a tangible or visible object but, rather, a pattern of sounds in the air or in the ear. That, of course, does not deny the value or virtue of printed pages, which I love. It is only to insist on what I take to be the essential nature of poetry, which is to be hearable and musical.

WEINREB: When did you realize that your commitment to writing was one that would sustain?

BERRY: I don't remember how much I thought about this when I was getting started. After 1965, when my family and I moved back to my home county in Kentucky, it became increasingly clear to me that I had a life's work to do, though not all of it as a writer.

WEINREB: How do you think other young writers should gain entry, so to speak? Do you believe in writing workshops—or in study alone?

BERRY: The only entry that is worth anything is the one into the attention of readers. But then, of course, that is not worth anything unless the work is worth something. How do you know if your work is worth something? I guess you had better not ever be too sure. A more practical, more interesting question is: How do you make your work better than it is?

For that, my own experience suggests that you have got to have teachers, a teacher being anybody at all who can tell you how to do better. I have been extremely fortunate in finding teachers, in school and out. Whether or not a teacher or workshop is worth anything depends on what and how well they teach. Writing teachers and writing workshops are wrong, in my opinion, if they exaggerate the importance of being a writer (something easy to do), or offer uncritical encouragement, or debase workmanship, or promote specialization, or promise some version of "success." The teaching of writing would be much sounder, I think, if its ideal product was not a published writer but an excellent reader.

WEINREB: Was there an emphasis on oral tradition in your family? Poems like "The Handing Down" suggest to me that there was.

BERRY: Almost all my elders have had stories to tell. My mother's father, whom I was lucky to know for thirty years, remembered a lot of local and family stories and told them well. Both of my grandmothers lived with their mothers-in-law, and I heard a good many family stories that came down that way: from mother-in-law to daughter-in-law to grandson. I have learned many stories from my parents and other relatives and from friends. I grew up listening, and loving to listen, to old stories and talk of old times. And that, of course, has influenced me profoundly, as a writer and as a man.

WEINREB: Sometimes in your poetry I hear the voice of a boy among men. Even the dead figure into your work often as role models. The persona in your poems, like all of us, I suppose, must face them and, ultimately, try to live up to their expectations for him. In fact, they seem to be, along with the living, simply part of the community.

BERRY: My answer here, I suppose, is simply yes. If community life is much a part of one's experience, then one's imaginative life is going to involve elders, predecessors, mentors, and these will include dead people and more and more dead people, the older one gets.

WEINREB: In reading your work, one cannot overlook your attention to death—especially to the idea that the mind ripens as the body decays. Like many poets of the past, you consider death from the focus of life's vigor. Will you comment on or explain your attention to it?

BERRY: One of the more idiotic questions that we now have to decide is whether or not we think death is a disease. If we think it is a disease, then we must oppose it at all costs, a line of work no more promising for mortals now than it has ever been, but extremely profitable for the medical industry. If we don't think death is a disease, then we must come to terms with it. I regard my attention to the matter as merely normal.

WEINREB: What did you read as a child? What of it has stayed with you?

BERRY: My mother read to me and encouraged me to read. To be sick and home from school and feeling well enough to listen was an excellent pleasure, because she would read to me. She read me the stories of King Arthur and Robin Hood, and *Swiss Family Robinson*, which I remember particularly, but many other things too. After I could read, I read and re-read *Swiss Family Robinson* on my own. I would get so fond of one book or another that I would read it over and over again. I read *The Yearling* that way, and Mark Twain's "boys' books," and Mary O'Hara's *My Friend Flicka* and *Thunderhead*. In high school, in class and on my own, I first read Shakespeare, Jane Austen, Hardy, Dickens, Thackeray, Thoreau, and began reading the poets. I read by spells and not very competently. And I've put down here just what I can remember offhand.

WEINREB: Will you discuss your early models and influences? Whom did you imitate as a young writer?

BERRY: This is very hard to know about. As a child I heard a lot of the Bible, a lot of hymns, a lot of sermons, and a lot of storytelling, joking, and talk, both black and white. All of this was influential. I'm wary of trying to deal with the issue of literary influences, because of my fear that I won't remember them all and my suspicion that I don't even know them all. Maybe it would be enough to say that after I began to understand my work as necessarily centered about one place, I have been very much dependent upon the work of predecessors whose work was similarly "placed": Thoreau, Hardy, Sarah Orne Jewett, Faulkner, Williams, Jane Austen, Gilbert White, Fabre. That is an acknowledgment of a special kind of debt. My influences are much more numerous than that, as I think my work makes evident enough. As I have got older, the older poets have meant more and more to me: Homer, Dante, Spenser, Shakespeare, Milton, Marvell, Herbert, Pope.

WEINREB: In "The Specialization of Poetry," you wrote of the need for writers to return to the real world in their poetry—a world in which values are not dated by fashion and older writers live on into the present with the values that endure. As you have done elsewhere, you mention the importance of "necessity," which precedes right action in the world. But what is the "mystery"?

BERRY: In that passage I'm not using the word in a theological sense. I mean by it simply everything we don't know. It is now more or less routine, I think, to fear that humans won't acquire or understand human knowledge. But even more fearful, to me, is the human failure to understand human ignorance. Not to know that we are ignorant, or to feel it, is to be dangerous, the danger increasing in direct proportion to whatever power an individual may have. "A little learning is a dangerous thing," Pope said, and our history has begun to suggest that "a little learning" means any amount that a human may have. From a human point of view, the difference between the mind of a human and that of a mountain goat is wonderful; from the point of view of the infinite ignorance that surrounds us, the difference is not impressive. Indeed, from that point of view, the goat may have the better mind, for he is more congenially adapted to his place, and he would not endanger his species or his planet for the sake of an idea. As I see it, then, the condition of mystery inescapably implies the necessity of restraint. The great events of our era may all have to do with the democratization of aristocratic vices. We have now completed the democratization of ostentation and hedonism, and we are well advanced in the democratization of hubris. A lot of people are now acting on the assumption that they are gods. Industrial acts of power that seem ordinary to us would have astonished Zeus. The Pentagon and the Kremlin have far outmoded Milton's war in Heaven. Dabblers in atoms, genes, toxic chemicals, social, psychological, and anatomical engineering all have promoted themselves far above their intelligence. One must hope for the democratization of a fear appropriate to the danger, and of a courage appropriate to the fear.

WEINREB: You've reminded me of two comments in *Standing by Words*: that "reality is in the study of dependences" and that "always the assumption is that we can first set demons at large, and then, somehow, become smart enough to control them." Hubris is, of course, a denial of responsibility on both these counts. But more appropriate to what you have said, perhaps, is the way that you lash back at such misuse of human intellect in "Window Poems": "When the fools of the capitals / have devoured each other / in righteousness, / and the machines have eaten / the rest of us, then / there will be the second coming / of the trees."

BERRY: That poem seems a little wishful to me now. Our fate and that of the trees may not be so easily distinguishable. It is likely that in killing off ourselves we will kill off the trees, or vice versa.

WEINREB: A question a day, an answer a day, always in writing. Those were the boundaries for this interview. Questions and answers in writing over many weeks is an odd, or at least atypical, way to conduct an interview. What do you see as the advantages of this form?

BERRY: I hope that I have made fewer blunders and errors this way—though of course there is no way of being certain. At least I have said nothing here that I haven't thought about. If I had been speaking instead of writing, I would have been under pressure to speak too quickly.

WEINREB: Like all of the southerners I have met (and the one I live with), you see a sharp division between public and private life. Another native Kentuckian, Robert Penn Warren, has a public posture in relation to interviews similar to your own, in fact. His sentiments echo Burley's "It won't do to talk much about your business" in *Nathan Coulter*, as I think yours do, and he likes to confound the public. Do you suppose that your attitudes about interviews are regional?

BERRY: A writer inevitably makes public a considerable part of his or her inner life. I have never felt that that implied any necessary publicizing of *private* life. There are a number of good reasons to maintain a certain privacy, and chief among them is courtesy. One's life, after all, is not entirely, or perhaps not at all, one's own. One cannot publicize one's own private life without publicizing at the same time the private lives of other people. But a part of this courtesy is to the public, which ought to be presumed to be uninterested in the private lives of people it does not know. I do think that there is such a thing as one's own business. Maybe that is regional, but I hope not.

Letters,
Poems,
Reminiscences

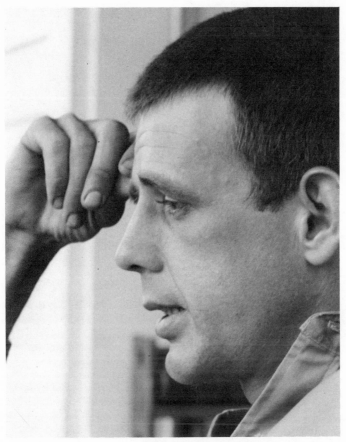

Wendell Berry, 1960 or 1961. Photograph by James Baker Hall.

Above: *Wendell with Den Berry, 1965. Photograph by James Baker Hall.*

Left: *Wendell Berry, 1967 or 1968. Photograph by Ralph Eugene Meatyard.*

Facing page, top: *Wendell Berry, Henry County 1970. Photograph by Guy Mendes.*

Facing page, below: *April 26, 1975, Frankfort, Kentucky, at a rally to oppose a dam on the Red River. This dam has not been built. Photograph by Pam Spaulding.*

With Mary Berry (now Smith) and Den Berry on the Kentucky River during the unusually cold winter of 1977. Photograph by James Baker Hall.

Facing page: *Two photographs of Wendell Berry, 1979, by Tanya Berry.*

Above: *With Tanya, March 1990.*
Photograph by Dan Carraco.

Below: *With Nick, 1989.*
Photograph by Dan Carraco.

At Lanes Landing, 1990, with Tanya and Doc. Photograph by Dan Carraco.

A Letter to Wendell Berry

Wallace Stegner

Greensboro, Vermont
July 25, 1990

Dear Wendell,

It has taken me a long time to write you about your latest book[*], and I know exactly why. I want to praise not only the book but the man who wrote it, and it embarrasses my post-Protestant sensibilities to tell a man to his face that I admire him. If I know you, what I want to say will embarrass you too, but we will both have to stand it.

Obviously I have not got through life without praising people—their houses, their gardens, their wives, their children, their political opinions, quite often their writing. But though I have liked a lot of people and loved a few, I have never been much good at telling them so, or telling them why. The more my admiration goes out to a man or woman personally, and not to some performance or accomplishment, the harder it is for me to express. The closer I come to fundamental values and beliefs, the closer I come to reticence. It is a more naked act for me to tell someone I am impressed by

[*]*What Are People For?* San Francisco, North Point Press, 1990.

his principles and his integrity than to say that I like his book or his necktie.

Nevertheless, though I admire this book as I have admired all of yours since you read the last chapters of *Nathan Coulter* in my Stanford classroom more than thirty years ago, and though I am touched by its inclusion of a friendly essay on myself, I want to say something further, whether it embarrasses us both or not. I acknowledge you as a splendid poet, novelist, and short story writer, and as one of the most provocative and thoughtful essayists alive, and I am not unaware that as a writer you make me, one of your "teachers," look good. My problem is that I can't look upon your books simply as books, literary artifacts. Without your ever intending it, without the slightest taint of self-promotion, they are substantial chunks of yourself, the expression of qualities and beliefs that are fundamental, profound, and rare, things that not even your gift of words can out-dazzle.

That gift, as Conrad says somewhere, is no such great matter: a man is not a hunter or warrior just because he owns a gun. When I quote you, as I often do, I am paying tribute to your verbal felicity, which is always there, but I am really quoting you for qualities of thoughtfulness, character, integrity, and responsibility to which I respond, and to which I would probably respond if they were expressed in pidgin.

Those qualities inform every page of *What Are People For?* They are fleshed out in the people you approve, such as Nate Shaw, Harry Caudill, and Ed Abbey. They are documented in your stout preference for the natural over the artificial or industrial, the simple over the complex, the labor-intensive over the labor-saving, a team of Belgians over a tractor, manure over chemical fertilizers, natural variety over man-managed monocultures. You reaffirm, in "Writer and Region," the respect for place that was evident in *A Place on Earth, The Unsettling of America, A Continuous Harmony, The Long-Legged House,* and other books. In humorously repudiating the speed and ease of the word processor you repeat your lifelong distaste for technical innovations that elevate the mechanical and reduce the human. In "The Pleasures of Eating" you carry your belief in natural wholesomeness from the production to the consumption of foods, and emphasize your sense of the relatedness of the agricultural and cultural.

Some people have compared you to Thoreau, probably because you use your own head to think with and because you have a reverence for the natural earth. I am not sure the comparison can be carried too far, though it is meant to be flattering. Thoreau seems to me a far colder article than you have ever been or could ever be. He was a triumphant and somewhat chilly consummation of New England intellectualism and Emersonian self-reliance. Emerson himself said he would as lief take hold of an oak limb as Henry's arm. You are something else. The Nature you love is not wild, but humanized, disciplined to the support of human families but not overused, not exploited. Your province is not the wilderness where the individual makes contact with the universe, but the farm, the neighborhood, the community, the town, the memory of the past and the hope of the future—everything that is subsumed for you under the word "place." Your "ruminations," as you call them, most often deal with matters that did not engage Thoreau's mind: human relations, love, marriage, parenthood, neighborliness, shared pleasures, shared sorrow, shared work and responsibility. Your natural move is not inward toward transcendental consciousness, but outward toward membership, toward family and community and human cohesion. Though you share with Thoreau a delight in the natural world and the pleasures of thought, I think you do not share his austerity, and I doubt that you will end, as he did, as a surveyor of town lots.

What has always struck me as remarkable about you, and hence about your writing, is how little you have been influenced either by the fads of *Tendenzlitteratur* or by the haunted and self-destructive examples of many contemporary writers. You may well have learned from the Delmore Schwartzes, the John Berrymans, the Randall Jarrells, the Sylvia Plaths, but I can't conceive of a time, even in your most erratic youth, when you were in danger of following them down. You never had a drinking problem or a drug problem; you have been as apparently immune to the *Angst* of your times as you have been indifferent to contemporary hedonism and the lust for kicks.

By every stereotypical rule of the 20th century, you should be dull, and I suppose there are some people, especially people who have not read you, who think you are. By upbringing and by choice you are a countryman, and therefore a sort of anachronism. The lives you write about are not lives that challenge or defy the universe, or despair of it, but lives that accept it and make the best of it and are in sober ways fulfilled.

We have grown used to the image of the artist as a person more notable for his sensibility than his balance. We might go to that artist for the flash of insight, often achieved at terrible cost to himself, but not for sober wisdom. I don't disparage those Dionysian writers; they have lighted dark corners for all of us, and will continue to. But I find your example comforting because it restores a lost balance—one doesn't *have* to be crazy, or alcoholic, or suicidal, or manic, to be a legitimate spokesman to the world, and there is more to literature, as there clearly is to life, than aberration and sado-masochism. Your books *seem* conservative. They are actually profoundly revolutionary, and I have watched them gain you an increasingly devoted following over the years. Readers respond to them as lost dogs turn toward some friendly stranger in hope of rescue. The thought in your essays is so clear and unrattled that it reassures us. Your stories and poems are good like bread.

I say that your books are revolutionary. They are. They fly in the face of accepted opinion and approved fashion. They reassert values so commonly forgotten or repudiated that, re-asserted, they have the force of novelty. In *What Are People For?* you quote some correspondents who are dumbstruck at your refusal to use a word processor, and your explanation of your refusal is as revolutionary as it is sane: you don't *want* the speed and ease of a word processor. You already, you say, write too fast and too easily. (You don't, but that is partly because you understand that a degree of difficulty is as necessary to prose as a scythe stone is to a scythe.) You don't want very many of the speed-and-ease facilitators of industrial life. You want, as many others of us do, to be able to work even if the power is down. You understand such things as word processors as the fences and walls that can collectively imprison us. You prefer to be free and at large, with your pad and pencil. But you want to be free in the place you have chosen, in the society of which you are a voluntary member.

From the time when you first appeared as a Fellow in the writing program at Stanford in 1958, I recognized you as one who knew where he was from and who he was. Your career since has given not only me but a large public the spectacle of an entirely principled literary life, a life not merely observant and thoughtful and eloquent but highly responsible, a life in which aesthetics and ethics do not have to be kept apart to prevent their quarreling, but live together in harmony. During the thirty-two years since we first met, plenty of people have consciously or unconsciously tried to influence the direction of your life. You tried the wider world for a few years, at Stanford, in New York, on a year's Guggenheim in Italy, and eventually you concluded that you belonged back in Kentucky, where you had come from.

That was a move as radical as Thoreau's retreat to Walden, and much more permanent. I am sure that people told you you were burying yourself, that you couldn't come into the literary world with manure on your barn boots and expect to be welcomed, that you owed it to yourself and your gift to stay out where the action was. I was myself guilty of trying to persuade you against your decision, for sometime in the 1960s I alighted at your Kentucky River farm and tried to talk you into coming to Stanford on some permanent basis. Fortunately, I got nowhere. And you and I both know of a more dramatic instance when you refused an opportunity that many writers would sell their souls for. You refused it because you felt that it might obligate you or impede your freedom of mind. Some might have called you stubborn, or perhaps too timid to risk yourself in deep water. I learned to think of you as simply steadfast.

It has been a robust satisfaction to me that, incongruous as you are in post-World War II America, little as you reflect the homogenized and hyperventilated lives of termite Americans, stoutly as you rebuff the blandishments of technology and progress and the efforts to make life effortless, you have won a large and respectful audience. You have established yourself as a major figure in the environmental movement, even though the environmentalism you promote is really stewardship in land use, and has less popular appeal than the preservation of wilderness, parks, and recreational land. You look upon the earth not mystically but practically, as a responsible husbandman, but your very practicality has made you one of the strongest voices against land abuse.

Those who read you devoutly—and this letter is an indication that I am one of them—find something else in you that their world too much lacks: the value, the real physical and spiritual satisfaction, of hard human work. We respond to your pages as victims of pellagra or scurvy respond to vitamins. You may lack readers among agribusinessmen and among those whose computers have already made unnecessary both the multiplication tables and the brains that once learned them, but you are a hero among those who have been wounded and offended by industrial living and yearn for a simpler and more natural and more feeling relation to the natural world.

And you give us all this with such directness and grace. Grace is a word that in fact I borrow from you, and it is the only word that fits. In an essay in this book you comment on two fishing stories, Hemingway's "Big Two-Hearted River" and Norman Maclean's "A River Runs Through It," the one "a feat of style" that deals with mystery and complication by refusing to deal with it, the other a work of art that ultimately "subjects itself to its subject." I like that distinction, for it helps to clarify your own performance. None of your writings that I know, and I think I must know almost all, can be dismissed as a feat of style. Everything you write subjects itself to its subject, grapples with the difficult and perhaps inexpressible, confronts mystery, conveys real and observed and felt life, and does so modestly and with grace. In the best sense of the word, your writing is a by-product of your living.

I should add that you wouldn't be as good a man as you are if you were not a member of Tanya, and she of you.

Yours,
Wallace Stegner

An Open Letter

Judith Weissman

Dear Wendell,

The invitation to write an open letter to you instead of an essay about you came at a good time: I had been trying to figure out how to thank you for the letter you wrote after I told you I needed surgery, without making you think you had to answer again. I always tell you not to bother answering, but you are too much of a gentleman to pay attention. So I am thanking you now. Don't answer.

There are not many writers who could get a letter instead of an essay, you know. It is not simply that I have the pleasure and honor of knowing you and counting you among my friends that enables me to say what I have to say in a letter; it is that I see no clear line between your public and private writing. The voice of your letters and the voice of your essays are the same.

Your poems are different. *Sabbaths* touches me deeply, but also humbles me—because I know I cannot follow you in all of your Christian faith. Perhaps some of your thoughts can only be expressed in these beautiful old-fashioned poems, which are not addressed to an audience whom you are trying to persuade, but simply say what you have to say about blessings. I grew up in and am in many ways still part of the scientific tradition that you distrust; and so these poems are still like a far-off light to me. I can see that it is light, but I cannot see it well enough to understand or identify it.

We meet in your prose. The patient Christ to whom you compare topsoil—that is a Christ I can understand. I do not need to list the ideas or quote the passages which have been important in my life and in my work; I have already done that in my book, and most of the people who read this will already know your work. What you cannot say for yourself or about yourself is what I want to say here: that your wholeness matters. Everything you write is about wholeness, about our need to restore a livable ecology in our farms and our communities and our families; you are too modest to point out that you exemplify such wholeness in yourself. Your life on Lanes Landing Farm, your essays, and your letters are all produced by the same human soul. You do not hand out advice to other people that you are unwilling to take yourself.

This sounds ridiculous, coming from one English professor to another. The last fifty years of literary criticism have been an attack on wholeness, a denial that it could possibly matter. Can you imagine what would happen if someone submitted a book on how a writer lived out his or her ideas to the Yale University Press? It would be rejected in fifteen minutes. I suppose that the separation effected by New Criticism was necessary, after so many years of genteel appreciations and pointless discoveries of minor biographical episodes that might correspond to passages in created work; to demand that a poem or a work of fiction be read as a self-contained structure was once a good move. That is still the way we all start, when we read anything. The question is not how to start but how to end.

Everyone got tired of the New Critical exercises as a goal. We could only discover and praise the orderly coherence of parts for so long. Both the old biographical critics and the New Critics made themselves so trivial that they laid themselves open for radical change—and did we ever get a change! If authors were discreetly avoided by New Critics so that the full beauties of a work could be seen, they are now bombarded, lambasted, and eviscerated as culturally constructed myths, incoherent pastiches of texts, as fictive and as corrupt as their works. Not only are we not supposed to talk about what might have led a writer to express an idea, we are supposed to deny that a person *is* a writer or *has* ideas. Now it is all "subjects" who "are written" and "texts" in the "lacunae" of which we are supposed to find the "traces" of what is not there, which is of course all we really want, since nobody ever wrote a beautiful line or thought a noble thought that we might want to discover. And we thought that the New Criticism had gotten tiresome!

But literary critical chickens do come home to roost, and the denial of wholeness as a value has led to the inescapable presence, in any big-time English department, of Paul de Man and Louis Althusser. They are the purveyors (along with others) of the supposedly enlightened, radical, revolutionary, "theoretical" new ways of reading. They have had so much power, in deriding "meaning" and hooting at "goodness," that their numerous followers are ready to excuse their personal faults with barely a blink. Althusser merely was declared mentally incompetent to stand trial after he strangled his wife; doesn't that have just a little to do with his repeated praise of "guilty" readings as intellectually superior to "innocent" ones? Would it be too bold to remind people that Pol Pot got his training under self-styled Marxists like Althusser in France? And what about the more recent case of Paul de Man, the prince of the Yale deconstructionists, a scholar's scholar, so they said—whose pro-Nazi columns an upstart graduate student discovered in some Belgian archives? At least this is being discussed, unlike Althusser's murder, which my graduate students have never heard of, no matter how many times they have been forced to read *Reading Capital.* As far as I can see, de Man's defenders are carrying the day, however; Derrida has informed us that to criticize de Man for his Nazi sympathies is an act of oppression as bad as Nazi genocide. So we had all better shut up and stop asking who this guy is, who told us that texts are all indeterminacies and slippages, non-referential plays of words for which no one is accountable. I wouldn't want texts to matter either, if I had written pro-Nazi columns.

They do things differently in rural Kentucky, don't they? You are at the edge of academia; there are not a whole lot of footnotes to your work in the dissertations being turned out in the most prestigious English departments. You may care, but you certainly will not change, because your life governs your work. Most of the followers of de Man whom I know are in life perfectly decent and kind (I cannot say the same for the Althusserians); but the connection is missing. The facts of their upright lives do not impinge on the insistent "deferral of meaning" in their work. Therefore I cannot quite trust them, for who knows when the work may overtake the life? But I trust you. I am sure you have your flaws, but I would be very shocked to find out that you had a secret life, a hidden self, some deep character trait that could negate what you stand for publicly.

You have had nothing to gain by answering my letters. No one is ever going to write my biography or collect my correspondence. You simply care enough about what you believe in to respect another person who believes in some of the same things. When I wrote to ask if I could please use some commercial spray on my greengage plum tree after larvae and brown rot had gotten every simple plum, you said you figured it was all right. You did not have to answer. You have consoled me recently when I had a sickness of the body, and several years ago, when I had a much more serious sickness of the soul. I found out how unfashionable your ideas were in universities when I wrote a book about women and agricultural communities in the nineteenth-century novel—and had it rejected over and over, before one brave, beloved editor took it. I lost count, but it was rejected at least a hundred times. One editor said I had to make it clear that I did not really believe what authors like Hawthorne and Hardy were saying. Since I had done my best to make it clear that I did believe it, I declined to make the required revision and kept going, and kept getting rejected. It was a murderously difficult time in my life, which went on for about five years. One of the few memories of that whole period that still gives me joy is a letter from you. I had described my plight and then said that at least my dalmatian puppy was learning to behave, and I had some peaches and plums on the trees I had planted; you answered that no reward which publishing could give was as important as bearing fruit trees and a good dog.

I seem to need a lot of consolation, and your books provide it, even when they are not addressed to me. I just reread the section on the tyranny of the idea of the couple in *The Unsettling of America*, which at least gave me the comfort of feeling that I had some company of the spirit. I am in a perpetual rage at being excluded from social arrangements made by couples for each other, couples who have had a perfectly good time sitting at my table, eating my food, and drinking my liquor. You are the only married person I have ever known—man or woman—who has recognized the prison that couples make for themselves out of sheer terror that a single person, if admitted to the company, might break up a marriage, and send one of *them* into the outer darkness of social ostracism. Everyone loses by the present arrangement, though most married people refuse to recognize the loss. Wouldn't the whole system be better if marriages were less self-protective and fearful, and if, in fact, there was less to fear? If single people were not shut out, married people would not be so afraid of becoming single, and might be able to look at other people as individuals instead of as pillars of society (couples) or dangerous firebrands (singles). Reading your passages on the pains of marriage as it is presently conceived did not change my life, but it made me feel less alone.

It is not easy for me to believe in the value of my own life, lived against the grain of academia and of the American capitalism of which academia is just a small part. The pressure to stop valuing my fruit trees and my dogs in order to be richer, more successful, more socially acceptable is so diffuse and so constant that I am worn out. But you are always present for me, telling me that resistance in life and in writing must go on. The future for people like us looks very dark, particularly in English departments, but stray, alienated souls do keep wandering through, helped by the knowledge that not everyone in the university is babbling about "author functions" and "the unconscious of the text" instead of human issues. A few weeks ago a woman graduate student in her fifties, who had been thoroughly terrorized by the "mode of discourse" in my department and needed a lot of care before she could feel brave enough to take her oral examinations, sent me a dozen roses after she passed. Roses are better than a letter as a message of thanks; those roses belong to you as much as to me, since you have helped me to have the strength to go on saying what makes me laughable in the eyes of my colleagues—that how you live and what you write should not be torn apart, that you should read with great suspicion the "theories" of someone who turns out to have been a Nazi son-of-a-bitch, that you should not stop using words that are now forbidden, like sincerity and nobility.

One of the reasons I sadly agree with your skepticism about education is that the very idea that a teacher should be a moral example for students is so "outmoded" that anyone who suggested it at a faculty meeting would probably be asked to seek psychiatric help. Of course we ritually pass resolutions on professional ethics, which ask that we adhere to some minimal standard, like not trading grades for sex; that is a long way from suggesting that those of us in the humanities, particularly, should take the virtuous sentiments expressed in what we teach seriously enough to try to live by them. Perhaps if more English professors chose wholeness, as you have, our students would not choose M.B.A.s as their next degree.

It does not look as if your way will ever win, but who knows? Last year who would have believed that we would live to see Alexander Dubĉek return in triumph? We may never have a moral springtime, but if capitalism ever has a human face, the face will look like yours.

Love,
Judith

Berry Territory

Gary Snyder

(Walking the woods on an early spring dry day, the slopes behind Lanes Landing Farm on the Kentucky River, with Tanya and Wendell)

Under dead leaves Tanya finds a tortoise
  matching the leaves—legs pulled in—

And we look at woodchuck holes that dive
  under limestone ledges
  seabottom strata,
  who lives there brushes furry back
  on shell and coral,

Most holes with leaves and twigs around the door,
  nobody in.

Wendell, crouched down,
  sticks his face in a woodchuck hole
  "Hey, smell that, it's a fox!"

I go on my knees,
put the opening to my face
like a mask. No light;
all smell: sour—warm—

Splintered bones, scats? feathers?
Wreathing bodies—wild—

Some home.

A Full Moon in May

Terry Tempest Williams

It has been a year since I last saw Wendell Berry. I can gauge it by the moon, a full moon in May. Abbey's moon. We met at Ken Sanders' home in Salt Lake City. We were gathered for "A Journey Home," the memorial service for Edward Abbey. It was Friday morning. We would drive down to Moab together.

We had chores to do like picking up the sound system so voices could be heard across the slickrock. Loading the six-foot speakers, microphone, podium, and electrical cordage into a white Subaru stationwagon was no small task. Wendell was strong, a man used to physical labor. His hands expressed the strength in his arms. The man behind the audio-equipment counter asked if we were involved in a rock concert. Wendell and I smiled.

"Depends on your definition of rock—" I replied.

We got in the car. Our job was complete. Driving back towards Sanders' home, we spoke of Abbey. Tender words. Private words regarding family, friendship, and the correspondence he and Ed had shared over the years. Although they never shook hands, their regard for one another was solid.

We pulled into Sanders' driveway, reloaded and packed the car, then hit Interstate-15 going south.

Ken Sanders, publisher of Dream Garden Press, is a big-hearted man with a whimsical beard to his chest and a ponytail that winds down his back. Wendell was in the front seat. I was behind him sporting binoculars around my neck, birdwatching from the backseat while Sanders drove.

As we rounded the corner outside Price, Utah and aligned ourselves with the Book Cliffs towards the town of Green River, the country became open, wide, and desolate. Clumps of sage stood their ground in the pale, arid soil. There was no hint of green anywhere, only the pinks, lavenders, and blues familiar to the desert. We said nothing while Wendell's eyes unconsciously searched for Kentucky. Sanders took his foot off the gas pedal as we approached a "slow elk" grazing in the sand.

"A cow out here?" mused Wendell Berry.

Sanders beamed. "Perfect rangeland, don't you think? Look at all this green grass brushing the bellies of these southwestern cows. . . ."

"More like brushing bones than bellies—" Wendell remarked as he stared out the window. "Cattle in the West—I had no idea. I understand Abbey better. I've never seen such a lean landscape. Its austerity is its beauty."

We travelled on, our windows rolled down. A golden eagle soared over the sage. I passed my binocs to Wendell. Ken stopped the car. Wendell watched the raptor. I watched Wendell. An eagle's size is not measured against other birds, but against mountains, mesas, and sky. They are absorbed into the country. It was only after the eagle's shadow passed over us that we acknowledged the face of the sun had been masked for several seconds by eight feet of wings.

A few miles ahead there was a road sign that read, "Eagles on Highway." Wendell was impressed.

"Western intuition." I kidded him.

We made a right turn at Crescent Junction with the LaSal Mountains in view. The rocks were red. The sky was blue. Moab was thirty miles away.

Sanders began telling stories of being stranded in the desert, one after another, a series of dreams or nightmares depending on one's perspective, like the time he and friends were rimrocked near the Maze in Canyonlands and eventually found their way to the Dollhouse days later, miles from anywhere—or the river trip down Cataract with Abbey when they lost their boat.

"Ed kept murmuring something about the River Styx . . . but we survived."

Wendell asked for some water. I passed him the canteen. More stories. I joined in—telling of the trip down Black Steer Canyon (later christened Bum Steer Canyon) where I fell twenty feet down the cliff only to be rescued by the arms of an old juniper tree.

"Buckets of blood—" I stressed in the telling. "And no help around." I showed Wendell the scar running the width of my forehead to prove it. "Beautiful country, though."

By now, Wendell Berry was catching on. He recognized he was in the company of two desert rats. And we were just getting started. Rattlesnakes, black widows, flash floods, and heatstroke entered our vernacular.

We began planning a river trip. Ken invited Wendell to join us. Wendell, a gracious and witty man, responded with cautious optimism, saying, "It sounds like a wonderful adventure, but I'll have to check my schedule for next year. It seems to me I may have a dentist appointment around then." His humor ribbed us as he tightened his seat belt, moved closer to his door and checked his watch. The window section of Arches National Park was visible on his right.

Ken and I had a plan to take Wendell to the Moab Panel, a series of well-known pictographs which hang above the Colorado River. We parked the car. I was wearing a red cotton dress and sandals. We hiked straight up the slickrock, the hem of my dress held in my hands so as not to catch it on the rabbitbrush and sage. Sanders knew the trail by heart. We climbed higher still. Wendell's eyes were on the redrock cliffs against a turquoise sky. Suddenly, he picked out the ghost-like forms. He stopped and shook his head. Ken and I stepped behind him. Wendell wiped his forehead with the back of his hand, rested his booted foot on a sandstone boulder and quietly said in his southern accent, "This is as far away from Kentucky as I have ever been." He paused. "As far away as I am ever likely to be."

We continued up the slope until we reached the alcove. Before us loomed large anthropormorphic figures—shamans, ghost dancers, ten, maybe twelve feet tall, painted ocher and red. We sat on the slickrock ledge for an hour or so in the direct sunlight. As shadows appeared new pictographs and petroglyphs emerged. Running mountain sheep and

figures with shields quivered with the heat. We were silent. Two ravens
perched on the cliff above us cawed. I cawed back. Wendell looked over at
me. I smiled. Ken smiled. We gave away no secrets. Wendell was learning
them for himself.

That night we joined friends at Pack Creek Ranch for dinner: Ken and
Jane Sleight, Brooke Williams, Sandy and Barry Lopez, Ann Zwinger, Jim
Stiles, Greg McNamee, Clarke Abbey and the Cartwright family. We had
gathered together to honor Ed. The memorial service was in the morning
at dawn. Many would be speaking. The full moon rose over
Tukaneekavats, a peak in the LaSals, translated to mean, "the last place to
receive the light." A few of us disappeared between dinner courses. More
individuals filtered outside, until a "Coyote Clan" howled recklessly.
Wendell was amused, then retreated to the porch after coffee. A man of
manners. And solitude.

I think of his poem, "Watching the Mid-Autumn Moon." It reads:

> Young, we had not enough
> respect for the changing moon.
> Then the days seemed to pass
> only to return again.
> Now, having learned by loss
> that men's days part from them
> forever, we eat and drink
> together beneath the full moon,
> acknowledging and celebrating
> the power that has bereft us
> and yet sheds over the earth
> a light that is beautiful.

Wendell Berry, a tall, lean man with knowing eyes, stole a moment for
himself. He sat down on an old willow chair and stared west towards
Canyonlands, now blood-red with reflected light. I watched him from a
polite distance. This was a man who understood what a deliberate life can
yield, what it means to be personally engaged in dialogue with the land,

physically as well as spiritually. One feels the rigor of his mind in the midst of his southern gentility. His ability to connect and concentrate in new country is his same ability to be rooted securely at home.

The next morning, five hundred people sat on the slickrock at dawn to celebrate the life and vision of Edward Abbey. We all looked for a circling vulture. Abbey's bird. Reports were made of one sitting in an old snag on the periphery. I believed the reports.

Wendell stood poised against the redrock landscape. An American flag snapped in the wind, as he spoke. He called Abbey a true patriot, "a man with a deep love of his country." What I saw as Wendell Berry stood in the Utah wilderness was a farmer, a statesman, Kentucky's native son. A man whose eloquence and elegance of mind has penned some of the most evocative and radical ideas regarding stewardship and the re-inhabitation of the Earth. He stood for community. His voice became his power as he delivered his "Manifesto: The Mad Farmer Liberation Front,"

> Love the quick profit, the annual raise,
> vacation with pay. Want more
> of everything ready-made. Be afraid
> to know your neighbors and to die.
> And you will have a window in your head.
> Not even your future will be a mystery
> any more. Your mind will be punched in a card
> and shut away in a little drawer.
> When they want you to buy something
> they will call you. When they want you
> to die for profit they will let you know.
> So, friends, every day do something
> that won't compute. Love the Lord.
> Love the world. Work for nothing.
> Take all that you have and be poor.
> Love someone who does not deserve it.

Denounce the government and embrace
the flag. Hope to live in that free
republic for which it stands.
Give your approval to all you cannot
understand. Praise ignorance, for what man
has not encountered he has not destroyed.
Ask the questions that have no answers.
Invest in the millennium. Plant sequoias.
Say that your main crop is the forest
that you did not plant,
that you will not live to harvest.
Say that the leaves are harvested
when they have rotted into the mold.
Call that profit. Prophesy such returns.
Put your faith in the two inches of humus
that will build under the trees
every thousand years.
Listen to carrion—put your ear
close, and hear the faint chattering
of the songs that are to come.
Expect the end of the world. Laugh.
Laughter is immeasurable. Be joyful
though you have considered all the facts.
So long as women do not go cheap
for power, please women more than men.
Ask yourself: Will this satisfy
a woman satisfied to bear a child?
Will this disturb the sleep
of a woman near to giving birth?
Go with your love to the fields.
Lie easy in the shade. Rest your head
in her lap. Swear allegiance
to what is nighest your thoughts. . . .

I closed my eyes and with the help of midday heat rising from the slickrock, imagined Wendell Berry giving his inaugural address as President of

the United States. Republican or Democrat—it didn't matter. Wendell Berry was leading the populace forward. I heard echoes of Whitman and Thoreau and I wondered why we don't follow the tradition of Latin American countries who recognize their poets as those who inspire change: Pablo Neruda, Gabriel Garcia Marquez, Octavio Paz, Ernesto Cardenal, and Carlos Fuentes, to name a few, have been ambassadors abroad and honored citizens within.

Wendell Berry is our nation's conscience.

A raven cried. My eyes opened. I returned to my body as Wendell closed with these lines:

> As soon as the generals and the politicos
> can predict the motions of your mind,
> lose it. Leave it as a sign
> to mark the false trail, the way
> you didn't go. Be like the fox
> who makes more tracks than necessary,
> some in the wrong direction.
> Practice resurrection.

Wendell Berry will refuse my nomination for President or diplomat. He will refuse my suggestion that he become Secretary of the Interior, saying he already has the job he wants. He is a farmer and a family man who writes.

But I will tell you this, one thing I learned about Wendell Berry in our brief desert travels is that the pen he carries in the front pocket of his work shirt is not a pen at all—it is a kaleidoscope, turned carefully by the calloused hand of a man who sees through the facets of American life his vision of health and strength between person and place.

On Cultural Capacity

Wes Jackson

Wendell once relayed to me a story told him by Tom Marsh, a potter friend of his. Tom had apprenticed under a master potter, a Mr. Shoji Hamada, who later became one of Japan's national treasures.

Day one in the shop, Tom Marsh was given the job of cleaning the toilets which included dipping human wastes out of the tank and carrying them to the field, sweeping floors, et cetera. For months this type of so-called menial work was all he did. Eventually the master did allow him to prepare the clay but even so, as the months went by, Tom became increasingly discouraged about the possibility of ever throwing a pot. But the day finally came in which Mr. Hamada announced, "Tomorrow you will make two hundred and fifty cups." Tom Marsh was at the shop ready to go by six the next morning. He worked feverishly. He skipped his morning tea break, skipped lunch, skipped the afternoon tea, and was going full bore when everyone else quit at six. Tom Marsh was still working at seven when the master returned to the shop and asked how many cups he had made. Tom replied that the number stood at 239, eleven short of the required, whereupon the master took each plank which supported several cups, carried it over to the area from which the material had come and dumped them all, all 239. Shoji Hamada then turned to his young apprentice and said, "Perhaps tomorrow you will make two hundred and fifty cups." Tom Marsh, aspiring potter, was crushed.

Much later, Tom realized that the time would come when he could make 250 cups with ease and that the *art of the cups would reflect the ease with which they had been made*. No lecture was ever given. Shoji Hamada simply destroyed the cups.

Wendell would not have told that story had its many messages not reflected his own understanding of what was at work in the master. For Wendell, a major point is that *the cultural capacity is more important than the product.* In addition, the fact that Tom Marsh was required to clean and straighten the shop reflects that the master regarded the unexalted end of the work to be of equal importance to the art. The master's insistence that Tom master the ordinary was, in other words, a flat rejection that high culture is separated from the low.

Readers of Wendell's work know what he thinks of the modern world view that drudgery is to be avoided at all costs or left to lesser people. Had Wendell not held this view, his work would be more theoretical and abstract and, I suspect, more popular. But it would not be lasting. Anyone who has read his fiction soon realizes that he is never removed from the lives of the people about whom he writes. Whether digging a post hole, restoring a hillside or training a colt, one does it because it is worth doing.

The cup story is rich beyond the outline I have just supplied. Wendell has probably thrown away more good sentences than most of us could ever supply in a lifetime. He is able to throw them away partly because his proficiency with the language helps him be less concerned about being interesting and more interested in telling a story well or getting a message across with clarity.

Wendell is truly an authentic source for our time. When we talk on the phone in the evening sometimes, I am not surprised to learn that he has cut weeds with a scythe from under a half mile of fence that day or that he has dug a hole five feet deep in rocky ground for a large corner post. It is precisely because cutting weeds and digging post holes are not beneath him that he speaks and writes from an elevated position.

I have had countless conversations with Wendell by now and what is so clear is that he doesn't have a resevoir of lines so much as a source for them. Like the good potter, he has the cultural capacity. Good lines continue to flow from his mind partly *because* he has used his body.

One of the many times in which we were discussing the limits of modern agriculture in the face of the alternatives available for biological farming, I said, "But Wendell, those who defend industrial agriculture count themselves as hard-headed realists." "Well, Wes," he said, "a hard-headed realist is usually somebody who uses a lot less information than is available." He said that in one breath and then went on.

Another time I drew his attention to some of the old timers who publish hundreds of papers in their lifetime, scores of books, get by on four hours of sleep a night and live to be 95 or 100. Wendell's immediate reply was, "Well, they have to live to 95 in order to get enough sleep."

Those who treat Wendell's poems, essays and novels as beautiful cups will have missed the full measure of the man who disciplined himself to develop the cultural capacity. And who would deny that the artful way in which he puts his sentences together reflects the ease in which they have been made?

Essays for Wendell

Hayden Carruth

I write to you, brother, to tell you
that the young sycamore,
princely as a yearling elk,
is dying. The bedrock of this place
is too near the surface, I think;
the tree hasn't enough root-space.
Which is an observation, at best a reason.
But this is June, my soul is sore
to study such gracefulness, so well started,
sturdy and well-limbed, thirty feet high,
which now in the spring season
shows bare twigs and withered leaves.
How can I not feel downhearted
to watch the young tree die?

Brother, our family is pretty large,
you might say enormous,

and we don't speak to most of them,
and they don't speak to us.

———————

Two-thirds of my barn
fell down long ago,
long before it was mine,
collapsed, the rusty
roof-metal now flattened
on the ground. It is worn
out. The loose loft door
in the remaining third
sobs in the wind.
The barn looks perfectly
natural among the cedars
in the tall grass where
flowers grow—dame's rocket,
stitchwort, and buttercups.

———————

And yesterday my wife found
at the edge of our woods the flower
of the May apple, suddenly there
on the ground.

Two big leaves, intricately cut;
beneath them the six-petaled
delicate white blossom shut
from the sun.

We could not recall
having seen it before, either of us.
It seems the May apple
often does not achieve flower hereabouts.
Or had we been too dull?

In flowers and all its natural
parts the world has kept
delight. Last night when we went
to our rest, we clasped one another
against insomnia, and slept.
I woke once, near dawn,
and her arm still held me.

This morning I saw—and marked well
on the windowsill—
a jumping spider. Such
a pretty thing.
Its two front eyes touch
and are as blue
as my wife's lapis ring.

> *One cannot act well or beneficially in a place until one has understood*
> *its* nature, *precedent to human intention. Thus, in a country originally*
> *forested, the farmer must study the forest, because to be healthy, the field*
> *must be an analogue of the forest; in analogy its nature is remembered.*

On its steep hillside your farm once, eons ago
in nature's fierce competition came to stasis.
Trees, immense trees for your young region, held
the slope against the water's continual surge
carrying away the brown dirt to the sea.
The river down below ran clear. For even
early woodland hepaticas can hold
a grain or two of soil in the freshening season.
You've contemplated this many a time
in your walking and working—I know because
elsewhere I have too—and have found in it
propriety and the importance of propriety
in farming and in poetry. Then of course
you found decadence when the woods were cut—
those bleeding trees—and corn and tobacco

were planted on the hill. Your mythic river
runs muddy still, muddy and bitter. No
propriety in that. Yet your fields now,
after extraordinary labor—brother,
I do not know how you can have done so
much—and after extraordinary thought
and study, are secure, right with the world,
proper, and full of meaning, which is love
in action, as your poems are. And what
a blessing this has become for us all.

———————

My place is on a hillside too, and looks
over the Stockbridge Valley to the opposing
hill ten miles distant, a remarkably
green and fertile American dale. In winter
when the leaves are off the trees, I see
twelve working farms, their multi-tinted
meadows and pastures, woodlots and gravel-pits,
through the picture window next to my
computer. Leave out the army, leave out
all such aberrations, this is by my count
my seventeenth place in my life; I live here
with my fourth wife, who yesterday gave me
a watch that tells time in seconds, the day
of the week, the date and month, and I can time
a horse race with it too—yet I've been called
a "farmer poet." I'm not. Alienation
has been my life, even though I've spent
most of it living and working on the land.
Now I'm too old. I write blank verse (sometimes)
not from principle but because I like it—
the privilege of a crank. I trim my fruit trees
and vines, I tend my flowers, mow my lawn,

my hayfield is sown to Panama grass,
timothy, and alfalfa, my woods are
grown-over pasture with too many thorntrees
but some friendly ash and maple on the upper
side, basswood, hickory, cherry, hornbeam, locust.
Now the orioles in the dooryard have fledged
two offspring, and vetch and daisies and hawkweed
are coming in the field. Summer is here. I can't
do much to help it, but brother, I talk with it,
and what we mostly talk about is you.

————————

You wrote: "The god I have always expected
to appear at the woods' edge, beckoning,
I have always expected to be
a great relisher of this world, its good
grown immortal in his mind." That
was in *Farming: A Hand Book*, 1970. And how
wonderfully that idea works, your *expectation*,
like your *analogy*, permitting many
possibilities. I have expected that god too,
and I'm still expecting him, the joy
of the world like Pan or Sasquatch
risen among the flowers or in the pristine
winter morning with new snow on the mountain.
To you, as I know from more recent poems,
he has appeared. What a striking, original
event in any world but especially ours.
I am astonied, as we used to say, I am glad.
For you, he is. And I think for you he is also
a source of authority, what you wanted
all along, to make the system go. For me
the system goes by itself—not very well.
Last year a big asteroid missed us by only

a few million miles. Yet in marriage
the orioles possess, at least for this season,
what I would call "perfect authority," such
as one can know it objectively, with their two
fledglings, carnelian in the appletree.
Now the melilot has bloomed near the barn,
a fountain of feathery yellow, and its authority
has brought it all the way here from Transylvania.
As Edmund Husserl said, values are
the "objectivities of practice," properly classed
under the formal heading of "something in general."
Something. An existent. An objectivity of practice.
And an authority too, even from broken marriages.
From the orioles and the melilot one moves
among formal headings, searching, searching.
I am expecting the god any minute, somewhere
near the barn. I like your faith, brother, and your
authority, so beautiful and important in this world.

One comes to a new place
with marriage in mind,
a new light on the beloved face,
a further tone of voice
that one had expected to find.

––––––––––

"What is left is what is" —
a few more years maybe
(one wants to finish at least
some of what one began),
a few moments of the fizz
of dawn in the east
before I go to bed,
a few more nights to see
my way in the dark. A man

like me likes to describe
things, who knows why?—
how the sunset's soft red
lights the orange lilies by
the dooryard, their coarse brocade
as if under a pink film
of pure imagination laid
upon them—a consequence
none could have foreseen
though it can overwhelm
anyone. And once a tribe
of ancients did see it. How
they responded I don't
know, except in their sense
they knew it, as I do now.
Flowers in the light mean
beautiful changes. I want
nothing more than these
that are what is. How still
are the leaves in the trees.
How quiet are valley and hill.
It is getting dark. The ways
of the night are memory,
new and transitory.
We are very remote here.
But in your Kentucky days
and in spirit you are near.

———

Maybe the sycamore
will make it after all.
Its crown is thickening;
I think more dark than light
might show in a photograph.
And if it dies, come fall

it will make a modest store
of heat for this heteroclite,
about two cords and a half.

Essays
in Appreciation
and Criticism

The Writings of Wendell Berry: An Introduction

Michael Hamburger

It is in the nature of Wendell Berry's work to call for very little background information, least of all of a biographical kind. That in his life which is relevant to his writing is also part of it, either explicitly—in poems, novels, stories and essays—or implicitly, because in everything he writes he draws on the totality of his experience, the totality of his vision. It is his distinction to be all of a piece, with the whole man, not only the whole writer, moving at once, together. A central cohesion and wholeness are what his writing is about; and this—in an age when "things fall apart, the centre cannot hold"—is what makes it different from the work of those specialists in poetry, agriculture, prose fiction, anthropology, sociology, economics or even ecology who do not find it necessary to measure their interests, disciplines or procedures against anything outside or beyond their specializations.

I came to Wendell Berry's work late, in 1975, when a friend at Boston University, where I was a visiting professor, gave me his book of poems *The Country of Marriage*. Berry's first book of poems, *The Broken Ground*, had been published in England in 1966, but I had missed it in my preoccupation with a more peculiarly American kind of poetry that was in the process of breaking through, belatedly also, into British awareness. Yet *The Country of Mar-*

riage engaged so directly with other concerns of mine—concerns that had less to do with ways of writing than with ways of living—that I was won over. On a second visit to Boston in 1977 I was able to review his next book of poems, *Clearing*, and at least notice the longest and most thoroughly documented of his tracts on culture and agriculture, *The Unsettling of America*. Meanwhile I had begun to search for other books by Wendell Berry, including his novels. The more I have read of his poetry, fiction and essays, the more they have complemented and illuminated one another.

Although Wendell Berry's regional identity, as an American Southerner and Kentucky farmer, is the very base and basis of all his activities—"What I stand for is what I stand on" is how he puts it in his poem "Below"—and it is far removed from mine, I felt at home immediately in his work. One reason for that has already been touched upon—that Berry's regionalism is not eccentric or centrifugal, but centripetal, and therefore tends towards universality. Another is that, in looking for the roots of his own immediate culture, he has placed himself in a literary tradition not exclusively Southern or even American. Among the twentieth century poets to whom he feels akin are two, W. B. Yeats and Edwin Muir, to whom I owed much in my formative years. Of these two, Edwin Muir is the more unexpected and the more significant affinity, because Muir's poetry has continued to be neglected even in Britain, and that neglect has a bearing on Wendell Berry's practice as a poet. With Edwin Muir he shares a bareness and austerity of utterance that runs counter to almost all the current notions of what makes any one poet's work individual and notable. Richness, complexity and novelty of texture or imagery are among the expected attributes of outstanding poetry. Yet there is a sense in which originality means not novelty or idiosyncrasy, but closeness to the origins of all poetic utterance. It is in this sense that both Edwin Muir's and Wendell Berry's poems are truly and consistently original. Sophistication is what is conspicuously absent from the surface of both poets' verse, though both have wide-ranging and delicately discriminating minds, as their prose works attest. This characteristic of Berry's poems struck me long before I had read his own account of his poetic practice, allegiances and aims in his book of essays *Standing by Words*, published in 1983.

In that book Wendell Berry not only defines his position as a poet, but issues a challenge to the specialists—that is, to the majority, as dominant in literature and criticism as in all other fields—quite as radical as his challenge in *The Landscape of Harmony* to specialists in social and economic planning; and the two challenges are inseparable, because they spring from a single source. "The subject of poetry is not words, it is the world, which poets have in common with other people," he writes in his essay "The Specialization of Poetry"; and again, in his aphoristic "Notes: Unspecializing Poetry": "In contemporary writing about poetry there is little concern for either workmanship or the truth of poems—in comparison, say, to the concern for theme, imagery, impact, the psychology of 'creativity'—because there is so little sense of what, or whom, the poems are *for*. When we regain a sense of what poems are for, we will renew the art (the technical means) of writing them. And so we will renew their ability to tell the truth." He goes so far as to deny art that autonomy accorded to it even by the Marxist poet Brecht, despite Brecht's insistence on the usefulness of poetry, on grounds not the same as Berry's—though Brecht made a distinction between "autonomy" and "autarchy" in the arts. Berry, I am sure, would accept that distinction, agreeing that poetry must be free to tell its own truth in its own fashion. What he objects to in much contemporary poetry and in its critical reception is the autarchy or autocracy of an individualism that has cut itself off from community; and that is where his aesthetic and poetics converge with his thinking about culture, agriculture, social and private life.

As for the modernity that is confused with originality in our time, his rejection of it also links up with his questioning of the benefits of more and more technology and automation: "But what we call the modern world is not necessarily, and not often, the real world, and there is no virtue in being up-to-date in it," he remarks in the context of statements made by other American poets about their work; and more drastically: "It is a false world, based upon economics and values and desires that are fantastical—a world in which millions of people have lost any idea of the materials, the disciplines, the restraints, and the work necessary to support human life, and have thus become dangerous to their own lives and to the possibility of life." Because it was in the Romantic period, at the time of the First Industrial Revolution in Europe, that individualism began to hypertrophy to the point of autarchy, Berry's fullest account of the poetic tradition— "Poetry and Place" in the same collection—favours those poets from Dante to Spenser, Shakespeare, Milton and even Dryden and Pope, in whom he finds decorum, good sense, a balance between the values of culture and those of wildness or wilderness—the very subject of his lectures on our own immediate alternatives. In a poem by Shelley, on the other hand, Berry finds a characteristic analogy with the unreal, encapsulated verbiage of present-day technocrats, messages exchanged by expert commentators on the Three Mile Island nuclear accident. "No high culture without low culture," is the briefest of his epigrams in the book, and Berry's "motto." Here "high" and "low" must not be understood in terms of class distinctions, but in terms of material needs as against spiritual, intellectual, moral and aesthetic ones. Wendell Berry's constant theme is that the higher and lower activities are interdependent, that our low or material culture must be right if there is to be a higher one at all, because both cultures rest on subsistence and celebration. That is why he can go so far as to assert: "Perhaps the time has come to say that there is, in reality, no such choice as Yeats's 'Perfection of the life, or of the work.' The division implied by this proposed choice is not only destructive; it is based upon a shallow understanding of the relation between work and life. The conflicts of life and work, like those of rest and work, would ideally be resolved in balance: *enough* of each. In practice, however, they probably can be resolved (if that is the right word) only in tension, in a principled unwillingness to let go of either, or to sacrifice one to the other. But it is a *necessary* tension, the grief in it both inescapable and necessary."

The tensions, conflicts and momentary resolutions are enacted in Berry's poems and prose fiction, since both spring with uncommon immediacy from his life as a farmer and university teacher, husband and father, but also always from a sense of a wider community, its way of life and its history. Even the old ways of rural community, with their cooperation in seasonal labour broken only by brief rest or celebration, are not idealized in his imaginative writings, least of all in his early novel *Nathan Coulter*. True, even in that novel Berry does not confront the dependence of those ways, in the American South, on the exploitation of Black labourers, a dependence that continued long after the abolition of slavery and the dissolution of the old cotton, rice and tobacco plantations. He made up for that omission in his autobiographical prose piece *The Hidden Wound*, part of which is reprinted in his *Recollected Essays* of 1981 as "Nick and Aunt Georgie." Though included among his essays, this moving and delicate tribute to two Black workers to whom he was devoted in his childhood would not have been out of place in *Nathan Coulter* or his later novels. In *Nathan Coulter*, he did confront the violence that could erupt with little provocation in the male characters of three generations, down to the boy protagonist of the novel—a violence due to an imbalance between the high and low cultures even in rural, agrarian communities not wholly disrupted by market forces.

This brings *Nathan Coulter* closer than the later novels, *A Place on Earth* and *The Memory of Old Jack*, to some of its antecedents in Southern fiction, the peculiar madness and frenzy so prominent in the works of William Faulkner, Carson McCullers or Flannery O'Connor—with due allowances made for differences in the locations of all those works. That seemingly inexplicable, eruptive violence in men otherwise gentle, patient and self-disciplined has historical derivations traced by Berry in his prose piece "A Native Hill" (now in *Recollected Essays*), where he quotes an account of Kentucky road-builders in 1797 who, after strenuous drudgery, suddenly begin to fight among themselves with firebrands. There he relates the violence in those men to the violence of their task of road-building, itself the assertion of the colonists' urge to eradicate nature, rather than to live in harmony with it.

In the later novels and stories there is more emphasis on the gentleness, patience and orderliness of rural characters still bound to their land by love and care, so that they are sustained inwardly by a reciprocity and continuity that extend beyond their individual lives. Yet in all of them there are characters who do not fit into the pattern, who do not wish to own land or be responsible for its maintenance. These black sheep of the old communities—a line of drunkards or "loners" stretching from Uncle Burley in *Nathan Coulter* (1960) to Uncle Peach in the story "Thicker than Liquor" in *The Wild Birds* (1986)—are treated with as much sympathy, understanding and humour as the upholders, like Old Jack Beechum, of the order to which Berry is committed—a vanishing order. Of one of the surviving upholders of that order, Wheeler Catlett in "Thicker than Liquor," we learn that his need for money "tended as much towards substantiality as did his love for his bride"; and with that we are back at the heart of Berry's thinking about community and his two cultures, as about the illusory "materialism" that separates matter from commodity, value from price, and substitutes numerical abstractions for the sustaining realities. From time to time this central concern can become explicit in Berry's fiction and poems, as in the story "The Wild Birds": "What he was struggling to make clear is the process by which unbridled economic forces draw life, wealth and intelligence off the farms and out of the country towns and set them in conflict with their sources. Farm produce leaves the farm to enrich an economy that has thrived by the ruin of the land. In this way, in the terms of Wheeler's speech, *price* wars against *value*."

More often, though, in his novels and stories Berry makes do with what he calls "the community speech, unconsciously taught and learned, in which words live in the presence of their objects" and which is "the very root and foundation of language" (*Standing by Words*). Since most of his characters are far from being intellectuals, this plain diction is their appropriate medium; but it is also Wendell Berry's preferred diction in his poems. It is in his poetry, therefore, that he takes the greatest risk—not that of being misunderstood, but that of being understood too well and too easily, thus of being rejected both for what he says and for disdaining the ambiguities that would make for a "suspension of disbelief" in those who do not accept what he is saying.

As in his prose fiction, so in his poetry this plain "community speech" can convey straight narrative and dialogue, but also an almost mystical undercurrent that allows him to make connections between the concentric orders of human life, like that between love of the land and love between men and women, pervasive not only in *The Country of Marriage* but in all his imaginative works. So in his story "The Boundary": "A shadowless love moves him now, not his, but a love that he belongs to, as he belongs to the place and to the light over it." For the poetry books, Wendell Berry has resorted to the persona of the "Mad Farmer" to render some of his more recondite insights, as in "The Mad Farmer in the City":

> Wherever lovely women are the city is undone,
> its geometry broken in pieces and lifted,
> its streets and corners fading like mist at sunrise
> above groves and meadows and planted fields.

In another "Mad Farmer" poem he admits: "For I too am perhaps a little mad," and one takes that as being a statement in his own person. Yet it is the Mad Farmer again whose satisfactions include

> any man whose words
> lead precisely to what exists,
> who never stoops to persuasion.

That is why the sober realism of Berry's settings, plots and dialogues very rarely demands direct pointers to the author's own unifying vision and insights, which he has qualified and enlarged from work to work, as once more in *The Landscape of Harmony*, but announced a decade earlier in *The Unsettling of America*: "The modern urban industrial society is based on a series of radical disconnections between body and soul, husband and wife, marriage and community, community and the earth. At each of these points of disconnection the collaboration of corporation, government, and experts sets up a profit-making enterprise that results in the further dismemberment and impoverishment of the Creation." The rural characters in his fiction do not talk in those terms; but they embody the alternative to the same disconnection by what they are and do, as in the rhythm of labour and rest, subsistence and celebration, that is also essential to much of Berry's poetry:

> One thing work gives
> is the joy of not working,
> a minute here or there
> when I stand and only breathe
> receiving the good of the air.

Wendell Berry would be a lesser poet if behind his plain words and plain statements like this one there did not lie "heart mysteries," as Yeats called them, as well as tensions and paradoxes that the most "ordinary" of men and women can experience, without being able to put them into words like "The light that is mine is not / mine" or "When the mind's an empty room / The clear days come" (*The Country of Marriage*). This is the transparent simplicity at which Berry excels.

To those who accept Wendell Berry's basic connections, because they know and recognize them from their own needs and conflicts, he seems "a little mad" only in the persistence and consistency with which he has applied himself to resisting the dominant, established insanities of our age. Such whole-heartedness and single-mindedness have become so rare as to look eccentric now, when in fact they are the attributes of a securely centred, integrated awareness. That Berry's is also a self-critical one, open to correction (like his works) and scrupulous in its weighing up of interests and views opposed to his own, will be apparent to readers of his lectures, as of *The Unsettling of America* or its sequel *The Gift of Good Land.*

To trace the subtle modulations of manner and substance in his successive works would demand more space than I can decently take up here. Nor can I indicate the range of his poetry from elegy to song, from narrative to epigram, from historical commemoration to reflections on topical issues like the Vietnam War. Most of his poetry has been gathered into the *Collected Poems 1957-1982*; and most of his major prose writings are also available from North Point Press, San Francisco. If I have refrained from trying very hard to place Wendell Berry as a poet, novelist or defender of community values, it is because he has made the necessary acknowledgements to predecessors and to associates like Gary Snyder—one of the poets, incidentally, who preoccupied me in the Sixties, and one who has arrived at a position close to Berry's by a very different route, initiation into Zen Buddhism and an immersion in the most various cultural and religious traditions. That two remarkable poets so little alike in their starting-points and their ways could meet on common, central, ground, bears out what I said about the centrality and universality of Berry's concerns.

Until recently, in Britain the antagonism between urban and industrial society and nature as wilderness or wildness was not nearly as acute as in America, both because by far the greater part of the country has been cultivated for so long that most of its natural history has been conditioned by its political, social and economic history, and because few British people had lost contact with nature to the same degree as many urban Americans. In Britain, too, as in Europe and everywhere, the balance between the two orders—between the autonomy of technical or commercial enterprise and the needs of communities—has become precarious to the point of crisis, so much so as to threaten the future not only of residual wildness but of agriculture. (I write this in a part of Suffolk where tap water has to be filtered for drinking or boiling, because of the seepage of chemicals from farms, and where a second, controversial type of, nuclear power station is planned on what is still designated as our "heritage coast," while most of the older industries, crafts and skills of the region have been driven into obsolescence.) I can be no more sure about the potential effectiveness of Wendell Berry's writings in Britain than about their effectiveness in his own country, but I have no doubts about their potential appeal. For one thing, his imaginative work is truly conservative, in a sense belied by the political parties on both sides of the ocean that lay claim to that name; and it is also radical, in the sense of going to the roots, not in the equally misleading sense that makes it synonymous with "extremist" or "fanatical." (The root of a tree is one of its extremities, but it is also that part which nourishes and stabilizes all its growth.) For another, Berry's plainness and directness of language in the imaginative works keep them free from the divisive jargon of trends, "camps" and fashions, so that they are accessible to anyone who cares for the essential, substantial words. As for his testimony in the lectures, it is as urgent as it is balanced and reasoned. Even on that level of discourse, different in kind as it had to be from that of the fiction and poems, Berry's rare sanity and wisdom find their right tone, at once eloquent with conviction and supple enough to respond to the doubts of the unconvinced.

Wendell Berry
and the
Politics of Agriculture

Gregory McNamee

Wendell Berry, by all accounts a soft-spoken soul with the conservative bearing of a Southern gentleman, stands among the foremost radical writers of our time. He is not only radical in the secondary sense, opposed to the dominant order; he is, more important, also radical in the primary sense, one who advocates a return to the source, the unsegmentable *radix*, the root. In any event, that radicalism is hardly the sort of mantle a Kentucky farmer, occasionally a university professor and upstanding member of communities rural and urban, might be expected readily to don. But Wendell Berry has throughout his working life been a man of profoundly felt, sometimes unpopular convictions, unusual enough in these days of quietude and desperate accommodation to things as they are. He would not, I suspect, disown the adjective.

Mr. Berry's radicalism grows from a state of crisis, the generalized chaos of our day and its specific effects on the things that matter most to him. As a small farmer who earns his bread from restored land along the Kentucky River, a team of draft horses his chief technology, Berry stands against the industrial agriculture of miles-long crop rows and two-story combines, the dominate mode of food production in America. Berry's opposition to the corporate economy he called "a gluttonous enterprise of ugliness, waste, and fraud," voiced in such important books as *The Unsettling of America* and

The Gift of Good Land, has been constant for a quarter of a century now, and with it he has earned the support of many like-minded agrarians, not the least among them the Kansas farmer Wes Jackson and his colleagues at the Land Institute of Salina.

For all their good work, the crisis continues unabated. Our agriculture becomes ever more industrialized, its destructive manifestations everywhere. One is the rise of monoculture, the production of but a few "scientifically" selected varieties of food crops, and the loss of genetic diversity that has come with it. As a result of the demands of industrialized, standardized agriculture, for example, of the seven thousand varieties of apples that have been developed in the United States, only four are generally available today: the Delicious, McIntosh, Winesap, and Jonathan, a meager table indeed. (The journalist and food critic A. J. Liebling wrote half a century ago, "People who don't like food have made a triumph of the Delicious because it doesn't taste like an apple, and of the Golden Delicious because it doesn't taste like anything.") As with such machine-produced items as metal bolts and pencils, the rise of industrialization in food production has led directly to an impoverishment of forms, a loss of the necessary complexity that informs any art rightly practiced, a diminution of choice.

This agriculture has also led to a direct assault on Mr. Berry and his freeholder colleagues, the economic war on the family farm. The small farmer began quite literally to lose ground under the administration of Richard Nixon, whose program of subsidies—including, incredibly, payments for *not* producing certain crops—favored such agroindustrial giants as General Mills and International Harvester. Under the benighted administration of Jimmy Carter and his secretary of agriculture, Earl Butz, who urged the ideology of food as weapon, tax incentives that had previously enabled the small farmer to take a necessarily long view of profit and loss were summarily stripped away. (Carter, let us recall, operated an industrial peanut farm in central Georgia.) With the nightmarish eight years of Ronald Reagan's misrule came further assaults, among them the termination of federal assistance for such things as fuel-efficient equipment and the purchase of new seed, with the result that no person of modest means—with capital of under $250,000, say—could hope to make a go of farming. The loss of other forms of government aid led in the mid-1980s to an unprecedented acceleration of farm failures throughout the United States, with attendant foreclosures and the depopulation of many rural areas. At the same time, agroindustrialists received additional tax concessions, allowing them to operate on an almost risk-free basis hitherto unknown to farming.

"The small landholders are the most precious part of a state," Thomas Jefferson wrote in *Notes on the State of Virginia*. The 1980s saw a barely concealed repudiation of Jefferson's dictum. Driven from their often ancestral holdings, disenfranchised, hundreds of thousands of small farmers lost their livelihoods in the Age of Reagan, the destructive effects of which will govern the American economy for generations to come. What small farmer would not be moved to rise against the dominant order, with Wendell Berry, upon contrasting his present lot with the governing ideals of the republic, upon reading the words of Hector St. John de Crèvecoeur in the light of our recent history:

> The instant I enter on my own land, the bright idea of property, of exclusive right, of independence exalts my mind. Precious soil, I say to myself, by what singular custom of law is it that thou wast made to constitute the riches of the freeholder? What should we American farmers be without the distinct possession of that soil? It feeds us, it clothes us, from it we draw even a great exuberancy, our best meat, our richest drink, the very honey of our bees comes from this privileged spot. No wonder we should thus cherish its possession, no wonder that so many Europeans who have never been able to say that such a portion of land was theirs, cross the Atlantic to realize that happiness. This formerly rude soil has been converted by my father into a pleasant farm, and in return it has established all our rights; on it is founded our rank, our freedom, our power as citizens, our importance as inhabitants of such a district. These images I must confess I always behold with pleasure, and extend them as far as my imagination can reach: for this is what may be called the true and the only philosophy of an American farmer.

In the economy of waste and greed that dominated the United States in the 1980s, small farmers suffered disproportionately—not least in their loss of rank, freedom, and the power of citizenship, a loss so total that it can only be regarded as deliberately planned.

The crisis of American agriculture mirrors the worldwide political and ecological crisis generally. Where the dominant mode of the Euroamerican nineteenth century was expansion and subjugation, that of the twentieth has been wholesale destruction. During the 1980s, history will recall, the world's rainforests were destroyed at the rate of 18 million acres annually (for purposes of scale, the Amazonian Basin comprises about 700 million acres, three times the area of France). Thanks in large part to that assault, an estimated one million plant and animal species will have been destroyed between 1975 and 2000, the greatest mass extinction since that which closed the Mesozoic, the Age of the Dinosaurs. The planet's rivers and lakes, its atmosphere, its oceans are sick with our ceaseless nest-fouling.

The crisis rages, the logical result of late capitalism, of the reigning economics of the short term and the fiction of what Wendell Berry has called "undisciplined abundance": an ethic of nonproduction, the buying and selling of abstractions, the exchange of junk bonds, the servicing of foreign debt, the economies of extraction, the wanton use of nonrenewable resources.

As Mr. Berry has written on many occasions, emblematic of that destruction is the loss of the nation's most precious natural resource: its topsoil. Only eleven percent of the surface of the earth is arable; a great portion of that productive land lies within the borders of the United States, giving Americans a special obligation of stewardship, of shunning profligacy. But that obligation has necessarily been violated by the practices of industrial agriculture, with its destructive demand for overproduction, its refusal to allow land to lie fallow, to plow along contours, to treat the soil as a living entity. As a result, some thirty-five percent of the nation's topsoil—formed in geological time, the result of weathering and abrasion, of the decay of dead plants and animals, essentially nonrenewable—has been lost, washed or blown away. In the twisted language of the agroindustrialists, it has for a century been more "cost effective" to allow that loss rather than to conserve the soil, the occasional dust bowl be damned.

Of late, more than four million acres of productive cropland annually has been lost forever through erosion. Put another way, every bushel of Iowa corn costs two bushels of topsoil to produce. ("At the present rate of cropland erosion," Wendell Berry observes, "Iowa's soil will be exhausted by the year 2050.") Put still another way, it now costs American agribusiness ten calories of energy to produce one calorie of food, an intolerably misguided economy of waste.

At the same time, our producing class is daily assaulted by greed and undone by indifference, although history has repeatedly shown that the happiness of a society is measurable by the contentment and wellbeing of its producers, its economic and moral mainstays. And our consumer class, from Donald Trump to the kid at the neighborhood skateboard shop, comprises "probably the most unhappy average citizen in the history of the world," as Berry has remarked, lending perfect credence to Karl Marx's theory of alienation. In this machine economy, all connectedness is lost. All sense of vocation, of heritage, of tradition, is destroyed. In their place we have, in Berry's formulation, an economy, even a culture

> based upon disease. Its aim is to separate us as far as possible from the sources of life (material, social, and spiritual), to put these sources under the control of corporations and specialized professionals, and to sell them to us at the highest profit. It fragments the Creation and sets the fragments into conflict with one another.

In this culture of illness, the Jeffersonian ideal has been demolished. We have been betrayed by our corporations, our governments, our universities, by all those devoted to stealing wealth from the future.

Against this betrayal, determined to puncture the cartoon balloon of prosperity that floats above us, Wendell Berry works as a farmer, a poet, a novelist, a social critic. A prophet by accident, his eyes opened by the necessities of tilling a hardscrabble patch of barely arable ground and by the destruction of the small communities—Port Royal, Versailles, Westbend—that verge his world, Wendell Berry's writing has been the most influential body of agricultural criticism to emerge in America since the turn of the century.

Arguing against the standardization of craft and knowledge that industrialism requires—a mental retardation of sorts, provided by our public schools, the training ground for Horace Mann's "industrial citizen"—Berry posits that we can free ourselves from the machine "only by undertaking tasks of great mental and cultural complexity. Farming, the *best* farming, is a task that calls for this sort of complexity, both in the character of the farmer and in his culture. To simplify either one is to destroy it."

Yet Berry works in simple terms, returning again and again to ideas that would have been perfectly transparent to the citizen-farmers whose work informs the best aspects of our culture: Mr. Jefferson, Cincinnatus. His terms, a radical vocabulary, address themselves to the roots of our crisis. At the heart of Berry's moral universe lies the concept of health, meaning not the mere absence of disease but the operation of a balanced, nondestructive way of life; his essays on the Amish people of Pennsylvania and Ohio, a culture to which he has often returned in his work, offer a model. "An economy of waste," Mr. Berry writes, "is incompatible with a healthy environment." Not an environment that is merely unravaged by the extractions of the machine, but an environment—natural, moral, and social—that operates in balance, within bounds. Mr. Berry uses the term *health* in exactly the same sense that Thomas Jefferson intended in a passage that should be engraved on the facades of every Department of Agriculture office:

> [T]he proportion which the aggregate of the other classes of citizens bears in any State to that of its husbandmen, is the proportion of its unsound to its healthy parts, and it is a good enough barometer whereby to measure its degree of corruption.

Another central term is *propriety*, also a sort of primary balance, this one of size and scale. "Good agriculture," Berry writes, and here we may read healthy agriculture, "is virtually synonymous with small-scale agriculture." And again, "strong communities and strong local economies are identical." The concept of propriety carries secondary senses, among them an attitude of respect, even reverence, and a recognition of limits. It is in all ways an antihybris.

Responsibility stands as a third pillar in Mr. Berry's moral and political vocabulary. The government of a free people has as its primary obligation the protection of that people and its wellbeing, although in recent times we have seen that obligation repeatedly betrayed. ("Surely not many nations before us," he notes, "have espoused bankruptcy and suicide as forms of self-defense.") For its part, the citizenry has an obligation to keep that government healthy, honest, and fit to do its work; that obligation, too, has been betrayed through a politics of indolence and apathy. As the mainstay of ideal government—the government of the Founders, basing itself upon an educated class of freeholding producers—the small farmer, Berry would have us understand, has special responsibilities: he must cultivate not only the land but also an intimate knowledge of its ways and use, an attitude of attention and faithful care; he must act in all ways in defense of his way of life and work, for to do so "is to defend a large part, and the best part, of our cultural inheritance." In that defense, the small farmer not only claims his place at the root of democratic society, responsible for the most elemental of all work, the feeding of his fellows (and the continued economic assault on the small farmer, make no mistake, will lead to hunger); he also becomes a part of the land, its protector and steward, integral to its health in a relationship Ted Hughes, another farmer-poet, has admirably expressed in "The day he died":

> From now on the land
> Will have to manage without him.
> But it hesitates, in this slow realisation of light,
> Childlike, too naked, in a frail sun,
> With roots cut
> And a great blank in its memory.

Health, propriety, complexity, the defense of intelligence, reverence, at-homeness, community: these terms emerge throughout the body of Wendell Berry's work, from the early poems of *The Broken Ground* to the late social criticism, talismans in defense of a culture and agriculture worth preserving.

Mr. Berry's work takes its place in a tradition, political as well as literary. The poetry shows Berry's affinities with Vergil, Horace, Donne, and, in recent times, the Southern Fugitive poets. Consider Mr. Berry's lyric "The Farmer Among the Tombs":

> I am oppressed by all the room taken up by the dead,
> their headstones standing shoulder to shoulder,
> the bones imprisoned under them.
> Plow up the graveyards! Haul off the monuments!
> Pry open the vaults and the coffins
> so the dead may nourish their graves
> and go free, their acres traversed all summer
> by crop rows and cattle and foraging bees.

Written in the late 1960s, during a particularly mad era in American history, Berry's poem and the cycle from which it comes, *Farming: A Hand Book*, denounce the wilder excesses of the culture—transience, amnesia, the incursion into Vietnam—while celebrating the pastoral ideal; the exclamations could be Whitman's or Ginsberg's. Berry's sentiments reiterate those of another great social critic, the English poet Alexander Pope, whose "Windsor-Forest" anticipates some of the later poet's guiding themes:

> Be mine the Blessings of a peaceful Reign.
> No more my Sons shall dye with *British* Blood
> Red *Iber*'s Sands, or *Ister*'s foaming Flood;
> Safe on my Shore each unmolested Swain
> Shall tend the Flocks, or reap the bearded Grain;
> The shady Empire shall retain no Trace
> Of War or Blood, but in the Sylvan Chace,
> The Trumpets sleep, while chearful Horns are blown,
> And Arms employ'd on Birds and Beasts alone.

Mr. Berry, professionally trained in English literature, wears his poetic ancestry lightly enough; he stands in and with the great tradition. His agricultural and social-critical writings, likewise, reflect a more specifically American intellectual and political heritage that has been all but forgotten today.

For Wendell Berry, whether consciously or not, continues a very old argument in our history: whether the yeoman farmer or the planter should prevail. South of the Mason-Dixon line, the planter has typically enjoyed prosperity, his farms situated in choice plains or along soil-rich deltas; the plantation homes one sees spotlighted in such flag-waving journals as *Southern Living* clearly show the economic successes of the planter class. Perhaps not coincidentally, the planters adopted new technologies of farming as quickly as they were developed. The yeoman farmer, on the other hand, typically worked a croft on marginal ground—stony hillsides, briar-tangled ravines, dogpatches—with the simplest of technologies, horses and hands. (As Wes Jackson has remarked, "Good land makes poor farmers. Poor land makes good farmers.") He amassed almost no wealth, and he owed no one; he was culturally rich, but cash-poor. It was the planter's money and the yeoman's blood that sustained the South for the four years of the War Between the States, a relationship that bred little love between the two classes. Where Wendell Berry's allegiances lie is plain enough.

Berry's arguments against monoculture, against single-cropping, are also very old. Southern agrarian journals dating to the early nineteenth century, and especially at the time of Reconstruction, devote themselves to pro-yeoman articles "on the themes of increasing crop diversification, halting the wastage of the soil, and eliminating blind dependence upon nonconsumable crops." For a time such articles made a difference in actual farming practice; in the early twentieth century, Clarence Hamilton Poe's influential journal *The Progressive Farmer*, many of whose contributions prefigure Mr. Berry's essays, reached a circulation of more than half a million, and Southern farmers indeed diversified their crops, helped along by certain intelligent farm policies of Franklin Roosevelt's New Deal. But the mass-production by the Second World War ended all that; soybeans and peanuts—plantation crops—replaced string beans and corn in the early 1940s, and the agricultural balance that once obtained, however shakily, between planter and crofter has never since been restored.

Mr. Berry's subsequent themes emerge repeatedly in Poe's great agrarian journal, as they do in the pages of such radical grangers as Liberty Hyde Bailey, whose *Country-Life Movement* (1911) and *Holy Earth* (1915) remain resoundingly modern in tone and outlook. He has closer antecedents, however, in the work of the Twelve Southerners, the Nashville-centered intellectual circle from which the Fugitive Poets emerged. In the pages of their 1930 manifesto *I'll Take My Stand*, the Twelve Southerners sound themes that lead to Berry's recent criticism:

> Proper living is a matter of intelligence and the will, does not depend on the local climate or geography, and is capable of a definition which is general and not Southern at all. Southerners have a filial duty to discharge to their own section. But their cause is precarious and they must seek alliances with sympathetic communities everywhere.

Adverting to such themes as propriety, community, and responsibility, the words might be Berry's own; instead, they are Donald Davidson's. Nowhere in the pages of *I'll Take My Stand* are Mr. Berry's themes more closely anticipated than in Andrew Nelson Lytle's magisterial essay "The Hind Tit," a powerful meditation on what happens at every level—economic, moral, social, cultural—to a yeoman farm family once industrialism is allowed past to enter its gates. Mocking the conventional wisdom of agricultural-extension agents (who have often afforded Berry his foils), Lytle describes the constant pressures on the crofter to "be progressive, drop old-fashioned ways and adopt scientific methods," the disappearance of the small-farmer's dictum that "a farm is not a place to grow wealthy; it is a place to grow corn."

Once he has given in to such pressures, Lytle promises, the farmer can no longer practice or even defend his native economy and the culture it reflects. He becomes a cipher whose days are indexed not by the natural increase or decrease of the fields or the vicissitudes of the weather, but by the fluctuations of the market economy. He becomes not a freeholder but a wage slave, an actor in the great miserable consumer cycle hitherto confined to inhuman cities far away. His children demand more and more goods they do not need, goods that require cash, not a handful of seedcorn or a jug of molasses, in payment. The whole order of his work, his economy, and his life is overturned; he is absorbed into the machine. He becomes, in Lytle's words, "the runt pig in a sow's litter."

The natural cycles of life on a farm—and of nature—are, Lytle argues, fundamentally incompatible with those of industrialism. The order of the machine is logarithmic:

> Industrialism is multiplication. Agrarianism is addition and subtraction. The one by attempting to reach infinity must become self-destructive; the other by fixing arbitrarily its limits upon nature will stand.

Propriety of size and scale, the recognition of natural bounds: Wendell Berry would surely stand by these words.

For all their similarities, however, Berry cannot be too closely identified with the neo-Confederate Twelve Southerners; his penetrating condemnation of the racism underlying American history, *The Hidden Wound*, forces a distance between Berry and those who yearn for the stars and bars, and in any event, the Faulknerian farm world of the Nashville scholars can barely be found today, even in Possum Run, Alabama, or Blytheville, Arkansas. "The theory of agrarianism," the Twelve Southerners maintained, "is that the culture of the soil is the best and most sensitive of all vocations and that therefore it should have the economic preference and enlist the maximum number of workers." Yet we have seen the disregard in which small farmers are now held by the government they once sustained, the decline of the freeholding class to less than two percent of the nation's population. The times have changed, and the agrarian ideal has long since lost the day.

Just as theories of progress—Marxian, Comtean, Spencerian—are bankrupt, so should we shun too much fondness for a supposed Golden Age. Wendell Berry indulges nostalgia little, and his work remains properly forward-looking. Drawing inspiration from a great literary and political tradition, Berry has brought a conscience into the present, seeking our return to a healthy culture: "a communal order of memory, insight, value, work, conviviality, reverence, aspiration."

For all that, the crisis continues. Iowa topsoil continues to wash down the Mississippi River; farm foreclosures continue at an appallingly high rate; the chemically laden products of the agroindustrial machine continue to drive real food off the market; the character of the nation, an unhealthy aggregate of alienated consumers, continues to decline; the rainforests continue to disappear. But we can, Mr. Berry continues to argue, save ourselves. Time is a plowed field, and we can work its furrows again, correct its contours. There is still room for hope.

In the end, salvation will come only with a responsible agriculture, with a responsible economics that shuns the doctrine of the short term and the ethic of extraction. These things are all possible; Wes Jackson's Land Institute, for example, is spreading the gospel of the polycultural "domestic prairie" throughout the Great Plains, where farmers are noticing that, having abandoned their expensive machinery, costs are down and real yields are up. It is not, of course, only up to the farmers: "City people," Berry reminds us, "just as much as country people live from farming and therefore have agricultural responsibilities." The responsibility, among other things, to demand a free republic, a freeholder's state, an anticorporate democracy. The responsibility to demand a return to our roots.

And salvation will come only with the widespread recognition that for thirty years one of our most radical writers has been correct; propriety and health and community are essential, honor and restraint and intelligence are indispensable virtues, the complexity of the world and the farmer's— the hman being's—connection to it are inarguably superior to the superficially more comfortable simplicity of the machine and the march of mass production. We know all that, thanks in good measure to Wendell Berry's stunning georgics, his powerful essays on agriculture and ecology, his lively polemics with Earl Butz and the functionaries of the Nuclear Regulatory Commission. Having that body of work at hand, we have no excuses.

Now what remains is to cultivate our garden.

WORKS CITED

Berry, Wendell. "The Farmer Among the Tombs." *Collected Poems, 1957-1982.* San Francisco: North Point Press, 1985.

———. *The Gift of Good Land.* San Francisco: North Point Press, 1981.

———. *Home Economics.* San Francisco: North Point Press, 1987.

———. *Recollected Essays.* San Francisco: North Point Press, 1981.

———. *The Unsettling of America.* San Francisco: Sierra Club Books, 1977.

de Crèvecoeur, J. Hector St. John. *Letters from an American Farmer.* New York: E. P. Dutton, 1957.

Davidson, Donald et al. *I'll Take My Stand.* New York: Harper and Brothers, 1930.

Hughes, Ted. "The day he died." *Moortown.* London: Faber and Faber, 1979.

Jefferson, Thomas, *Notes on the State of Virginia.* New York: W.W. Norton, 1968.

Pope, Alexander. "Windsor-Forest." E. Audra and Aubrey Williams, eds., *The Poems of Alexander Pope, Volume I.* London: Methuen and Co. Ltd., 1961.

Wilson, Charles Regan and William Ferris, eds., *Encyclopedia of Southern Culture.* Chapel Hill: University of North Carolina Press, 1989.

Traveling at Home: Wandering and Return in Wendell Berry

Mark Shadle

Follow the microscope or telescope far enough and you reach a vast emptiness—the nowhere of near and far. Somewhere between these extremes, beneath constellations seen with the naked eye, is a human home. Such a place is delicately balanced at the heart of Wendell Berry's lifework, made of flesh and word (like the Chinese ideogram that connects a man and his word on the cover of *Standing by Words*). Creating and maintaining such a stable place takes a faithful act of will, curiosity, research and growing skills. Paradoxically, home is not only geocentric, but simultaneously a set of margins for Berry. Embracing the territoriality humans in some ways share with animals, he knows that home travels out centrifugally and horizontally through the household to farm and wilderness on the one hand, and to community, region, nation and world on the other.

The first imperative for Berry's writing, however, has been not out, but down and back—the gravity of a centripetal force (as Michael Hamburger has noted in his introduction to *The Landscape of Harmony*) that directs home through the body to the earth and back again. This defense of home is hardly surprising in our world of disintegrating communities and, perhaps, languages. In a growing body of essays, Berry has focussed down on the home by speaking for: a loving stewardship of the land as the first step

toward a better defense than non-specific nuclear weapons; an end to rapa-
cious and unsettling agribusiness and the return to the small family farm;
animal, wind and solar power over spontaneous combustion engines; marriage as counter to a rising divorce rate; sexual restraint as part of the cure
for over-population; and the importance of living hand to mouth and both
to brain.

Because words are not just tokens of a more ideal reality, but further
tools of a farmer-teacher-writer, Berry has carted home those that he feels
have been misappropriated. "Accountability" is stolen back from business,
just as household "management" returns as the real meaning of economics
and a replacement for Wall Street. Thus "home economics" becomes the
whole working of the house and farm, rather than the stereotype of a
chauvinist high school cooking course for girls escaping math. The work of
the amateur (its roots are in the word for love) replaces the centralized
competition between specialists with a diversity of ideas, people, plants and
animals. Small becomes beautiful, and the harmonious home a refuge from
dissonance, while ignorance is wrestled into familiarity and skill. A good
peace will outlast a chaotic evil. A disorienting jet plane ride is tolerated
only to pay respects (as Berry does in "Irish Journal" in *Home Economics*) to
an ancestral village.

Slowly an insistent vocabulary is built up and recollected in Berry's
writings. But his thought is not so much an involuntary insistence on
overlapping key words as a repetition chosen over and over—a concentra-
tion and concentricity that act like a magical incantation toward harmony
and peace. At the heart of these choices of ideas is the tension between
"travel" and "home." While this war of words (and their consequential acts)
is part of the privilege and limitation of the English language, not all of
these pairings are the seemingly-perfect contraries of good and evil. In
William Blake's terms, some may be opposites that are not true contraries.
Nature/culture, wilderness/city, war/peace and (especially) travel/home
not only interpenetrate, but are interdependent.

I know of no better or more curiously-disturbing exploration of this
complex and costly business of a full home-coming from traveling into
nature/culture in Berry's work than in his use of Odysseus' return in
Homer's *Odyssey* in the chapter of *The Unsettling of America* entitled, "The

Body and the Earth." Ever since I read it years ago, it has seemed shocking that Berry could accept, however guardedly, Odysseus' murder of Penelope's suitors when that Greek warrior returned home from war. Anyone who has seen the bloody results of reapportionment of land in the Third World(s) will want to take a close look at Berry's initial explanation in that essay:

> *The Odyssey*, then, is in a sense an anti-*Iliad*, posing against the warrior values of the other epic—the glories of battle and foreign adventuring—an affirmation of the values of domesticity and farming. But at the same time *The Odyssey* is too bountiful and wise to set these two kinds of value against each other in any purity or exclusiveness of opposition. . . . Odysseus' fidelity and his homecoming are as moving and instructive as they are precisely because they are the result of *choice*. (129)

The idea that evil is chiefly present to let us choose the good is still unsatisfying. In our culture, Odysseus would still be a vigilante or rebel, taking the law into his own hands to slay the suitors; so Berry provides a further defense when he says:

> It is made clear that the punishment is not merely the caprice of a human passion: Odysseus enacts the will of the gods; he is the agent of a divine judgment. The suitors' sin is their utter contempt for the domestic order that the poem affirms. They do not respect or honor the meaning of the household, and in *The Odyssey* this meaning is paramount. (126)

It seems that multiple acts of violence (Odysseus' killing of both the immoral suitors and immoral maidservants) and mock-violence (the feigned destruction of the marriage of Penelope and Odysseus when she orders the bed moved as test, and he angrily responds) are part of the hard truth that peace is born of division (which extends even to the gods and goddesses, who fight among themselves frequently in Greek mythology). Just as

Odysseus defended Helen's marriage at Troy, and chose mortality with Penelope over immortality with the goddess-temptress, Kalypso, he now must defend his own marriage at home.

Odysseus' moment of home-coming is precisely the time to stand by his living family and word, ready finally to exert, with presumably less interference from the soon-to-be-appeased and still-revered gods and goddesses, a calmer, more tolerant judgment as an end (or at least balance) to war (which the suitors have carried like a seed and reminder). Is not the gravity of his centripetal circling back to home already mirrored in the growth-rings of that olive tree that has grown out to meet him, sharing nature with culture as it has become—eloquently mute—a part of his bed? Is this tree, as wood, not still "flowering," making the bed more than icon, and letting it become a participant in the sexual and mythological re-unification of house and farm as "householding?" Berry describes such a possibility gracefully in the following words:

> All around, this structure [*The Odyssey*] verges on the sea, which is the wilderness, ruled by the forces of nature and by the gods. In spite of the excellence of his ship and crew and his skill in navigation, a man is alien there. Only when he steps ashore does he enter a human order. From the shoreline of his island of Ithaka, Odysseus makes his way across a succession of boundaries, enclosed and enclosing, with the concentricity of a blossom around its pistil, a human pattern resembling a pattern of nature. He comes to his island, to his own lands, to his town, to his household and house, to his bedroom, to his bed. (125)

Berry's essay is not only about the harmony and connectedness of society and nature, but also, by implication, necessarily concerned with pacifism and war. It is as if the reader must be reminded that the war Odysseus has fought so far "afield" began with a direct defense of his home and household, which are in turn settled (always a little uncertainly) into nature. His twenty years of war and travel would be indefensible as the pleasure of German wanderlust; rather, they are a true nostalgia (from the Greek *nostos*, or "return home"). In Webster's this word has evolved into a meaning Homer and Berry might not accept, making it into the "home*sickness*" that is "an abnormal yearning for return to or of some past period or irrecoverable condition." Odysseus means to have a full recovery, minus the years he was away.

But in this view that sees him absent from home as warrior and wanderer, he is symbolic of violence and disunity in our industrial world. Lost from his home and even fellow soldiers, Odysseus is the isolated individual we first see not just as our two hundred thousand homeless children, or many more "latch-key" kids, but as the majority of our young, who spend more time in front of TV than in school. As Berry notes in "Getting Along with Nature" (in *Home Economics* 15), such a figure cannot be defined: "The Chain of Being, for instance—which gave humans a place between animals and angels in the order of Creation—is an old idea that has not been replaced by any adequate new one. It was simply rejected, and the lack of it leaves us without a definition."

American popular culture has a surprising number of examples of stranded farmer-turned-warrior characters. Even though they fight for a notion of home and staying put, they seem to lack this sense of possible Odyssean transcendence or definition mentioned above. In the film, *Mr. Majestyk*, Charles Bronson plays a rancher unafraid of bucking the local rednecks, who terrorize the Mexican-American migrant workers he is eager to hire. In spite of some back-and-forth violence and threats, he attempts to stay tuned to his harvest of melons. However, when these same folks try to kill Bronson and his migrant-worker lover, he reverses roles by surrounding, then eliminating, them through his better "natural attributes" of tracking, baiting and hunting. More recently, *The Milagro Beanfield War*—another popular book that became a movie—describes a similar process.

Philosopher J. Glenn Gray, when writing a personal account of the effects of The Second World War on his life in *The Warriors*, may have given us a way of understanding the violent retaliation of both the Mr. Majestyk played by Charles Bronson (who protects his lover and melons), and Odysseus (who protects his wife and bed) when he wrote in 1959:

> He [modern man] knows full well that he can be no proper
> god, for he is filled with a longing for something or someone
> to whom to belong. In the face of an overpowering universe, he

realizes, consciously or not, that his freedom and independence are relative and puny. What is missing so often in modern men is a basic piety, the recognition of dependence on the natural realm. . . .

This separation of man from nature as a consequence of our too-exclusive interest in power is in part responsible for the total wars of our century. More than we ever realize, we have transferred our exploitative attitudes from nature to man. In total war, men become so much material, and civilian populations, like soldiers, have to be ravaged and subdued. Distinctions between innocent and guilty, the permissible and prohibited, become extinguished. Men and machines approach each other more nearly. The most painful impressions of World War II for me . . . were the ruthless trampling down of the works of nature and the innocent products of human art. . . . The butchering of each other was almost easier to endure than the violation of animals, crops, farms, homes, bridges, and all the other things that bind man to his natural environment and help to provide him with a spiritual home. (237-8)

Berry admits that he is "not by principle a passive man, or by nature a pacific one" in "Property, Patriotism, and National Defense" (in *Home Economics* 100). Yet he echoes Gray's thoughts above when he says, in the same essay:

When urban property is gathered into too few hands and when the division between owners and users becomes therefore too great, a sort of vengeance is exacted upon urban property: people litter their streets and destroy their dwellings. When rural property is gathered into too few hands, even when, as in farming, the owners may still be the users, there is an inevitable shift of emphasis from maintenance to production, and the land deteriorates. (106-7)

Thus it is appropriate that the thugs after Bronson and his "hired hands" act more like machines ("hired guns"), hoping that the rapid firing of their machine guns will make up for any lack of good aim with a weapon or in their lives. With no stake or pride in the countryside, these gunmen litter the countryside with bullets, shooting indiscriminately at people, house, barn and melons.

If this absence of religious sensitivity or transcendence is one contributor to disharmony, the American tradition of dispersal and displacement is another. Odysseus has not, like those purgatorial souls who symbolize contemporary man living vicariously and dangerously through the lives of others at sea in the "jungle" of a big city, lost the memory or vision of his home. Yet is he free of both the stain and training of the exploratory and colonizing instincts which Berry calls the "unsettling" of America (where no Native American tribe seems to have had an equivalent for our word, "wild," as "other")? In *The Invention of America*, Edmund O'Gorman reaffirms this notion that "not every finding is a discovery," and that we see only what we are looking for. Columbus, he explains, (re-)"discovered" the New World only because of a well-known story of the "autonomous pilot" current in the Europe of his day. And Loren Eiseley underscores the importance of remaining open to the new in *The Unexpected Universe* with an epigraph from Heraclitus: "If you do not expect it, you will not find the unexpected, for it is hard to find and difficult." In the title essay, Eiseley claims that each of us may carry within ourself a "ghost continent—a place circled as warily as Antarctica was circled two hundred years ago by Captain James Cook" (3). Without his vision of home, and a will to return there, Odysseus is like the scientist reporting the "small story of an observer lost upon the fringes of large events" (3). Eiseley hints at the importance of this mix of will and curiosity to set a literary tone when he says: "Let it be understood that I claim no discoveries. I claim only the events of a life in science as they were transformed inwardly into something that was whispered to Odysseus long ago" (3).

Eiseley goes on to speak even more directly about the relevance of *The Odyssey* to our recent past (the late 1960's):

> Odysseus' passage through the haunted waters of the eastern
> Mediterranean symbolizes, at the start of the Western intellec-
> tual tradition, the sufferings that the universe and his own
> nature impose upon homeward-yearning man.

> In the restless atmosphere of today all the psychological elements of the *Odyssey* are present to excess: the driving will toward achievement, the technological cleverness crudely manifest in the blinding of Cyclops, the fierce rejection of the sleepy Lotus Isles, the violence between man and man. Yet, significantly, the ancient hero cries out in desperation, "There is nothing worse for men than wandering." (4-5)

Most American children still learn that the Pilgrims had already been several times displaced—from England to Holland and back—before coming to the New World; however, few of them are taught to appreciate the possible significance of this. These same children rarely learn that the Pilgrims could escape from those intolerant of them, but not from themselves and the seeds they carried for their own destruction, even in their language. In America they—and other colonists who followed them, religious and secular—were left too alone, and turned against the Native Americans whom they lumped together with nature (when they were not busy dreaming of The Garden of Eden) as "howling wilderness." A whole host of literary studies portray America as a vulnerable woman (Henry Nash Smith's *The Virgin Land*, 1955) raped (Leo Marx's *The Machine in the Garden*, 1962) until we feed on violence (Richard Slotkin's *Regeneration Through Violence*, 1971). The facts and perspectives of these earlier myth and symbol books are carried forward into the often-disastrous effects of big agribusiness on the soil and farmers of America in our time in Berry's excellent account of *The Unsettling of America* (1977).

The first moral, here—that not only sticks and stones, but also the languages and myths fashioned of words are dangerous—is bad enough. But the second may be even more troubling: starting over in a new environment is a grueling choice between remaining flexible by looking for and interacting with the unexpected on the one hand, or blindly holding onto the "old ways" on the other. Edward Hoagland, a contemporary member of those restless travelers out of the temperate zones to more exotic climes, claims that many Americans abroad suffer not from the need of groups like the Pilgrims or Puritans to maintain their established customs, but rather from a lust for novelty and a need for a too-perfect human understanding that falls short of a spiritual one. At the beginning of his essay, "The Light from the Snake on the Mountain" (in *African Calliope*, 1979), he says:

> After one has read dozens of explorers' journals, with the books of contemporary wilderness enthusiasts thrown in, it isn't hard to reach the conclusion that the search these individuals have made to find the wildest areas left on earth—a kind of relay race, at best, but a lone compulsion in many cases—was really an attempt, itself, to start over. I'm not speaking of formal anthropology, but of the impetus of so much wilderness trekking and love-of-the-primitive, the wish to go and live in the bosom of raw nature. A fist-fighter lurks just under the surface of a lot of these books. The masochism or sadism, the general tenor of choler, vainglory and self-distrust so often perceptible between the lines makes you suspect that one reason why the author sought so hard for a personal, presumptive site for the birth of man, and a feel for the circumstances of it, was that he wanted to be born again, to reexperience his own birth and thereby possibly straighten himself out—to *do things over*. (70-71)

Even if the self-exiled American were not intent on starting over, s/he might want to travel to avoid society. One of my colleagues suggests, only half-facetiously, that the muggers and child-molesters of our cities used to be able to head off to Alaska or the Yukon, but have no equivalent access to our current "last frontier" in outer space. While this notion of displacement in a shifting geographical or emotional frontier-as-safety-valve is not new, it increasingly disturbs us as we begin to equate those exiled abroad to those lost in our largest cities. Can we be sure that the self-exiled explorer, aware of the ghost continent within her or himself, and with an apocalyptic, idealistic or millennialist impulse to start over, is taking a different path from the contented small farmer who stays at home, "within the fold?" Do good farmers merely smile on their inheritance, or may they also grow from resistance?

The best of travel lets us get away from home not necessarily to emigrate, start over or escape, but to put home in perspective. In this sense, even the small farmer may have his own version of vision quest. Masanobu Fukuoka, whose introduction to America Wendell Berry speeded, with his preface to that enfolded little gem of a book, *The One-Straw Revolution*, reports how he had to go through an involuntary emotional break-down in a large Japanese city in order to break down his scientific research of plants into the loving practice of planting. Only then could he "organically-grow" the little farm close to his home village. His story joins so many others in what mythologist Joseph Campbell, in *The Hero With A Thousand Faces*, describes as central: the hero who goes through physical and emotional trials in order to return to a life of harmony and usefulness.

Does our very language necessarily seek confusion between our seemingly-contrary impulses to peace and order on the one hand, and restlessness and chaos on the other? If the explorers whom Hoagland and Eiseley both write about are escaping into *circular* voyages to avoid their past lives, they are also trying to *straighten themselves out*. Is this difference one between a matriarchal and patriarchal navigation, or perhaps between cyclical and linear cultures?

How far apart, psychologically speaking, are violence and estrangement from the feeling of "being at home in the world?" Excited by my reading of Charles Olson's poetry and essays, I re-read Professor Gray's *The Warriors* (mentioned earlier) and found an attention to a passage from Heraclitus that Olson frequently repeated, and is quoted below both as the simultaneous beginning of a healing of war, but also its mystery:

> The ancient Greek philosopher Heraclitus once wrote that "men are estranged from what is most familiar and they must seek out what is in itself evident." The sentence illuminates, as few others have done, much of my own war experience. The atmosphere of violence draws a veil over our eyes, preventing us from seeing the plainest facts of our daily existence. To an awakened conscience, everything about human actions becomes then strange and nearly inexplicable. Why men fight without anger and kill without compunction is understandable at all only to a certain point. A slight alteration in conscious-

ness would be sufficient to put their deeds in a true light and turn them forever from destruction. It would require only a coming to themselves to transform killers into friends and lovers, for, paradoxical as it may seem, the impulses that make killers are not so different in kind from those that make lovers. I know no other explanation for the notorious linkage in war between the noblest and basest deeds, the most execrable vices and the sublimest virtues.

The feeling of being at home in the world is likewise not much removed from the feeling of being exposed and hopelessly lost to all succor. . . . The change in us from the one state of being to the other is, of course, profound, but the psychological distance to traverse is slight. Most of us have known both extremes, often in an incredibly short span of time. It is as though a thin but impenetrable wall separated the two states. If at moments the wall seems easily torn away, usually it proves to be more durable than our lives. (232-33)

As the bricks, cement and barbed-wire of the Berlin Wall have begun to be removed this year, Germans on both sides seem a little confused about what to do, and where to go. It is as if Gray's invisible wall and Loren Eiseley's ghost continent remain firmly in place. Such barriers have been interiorized as symbols of multiple battles, and cannot be flattened or forgotten easily in a few days. Even if, as Gray says above, the psychological distance between East and West Germany may be slight, the ghost of the Berlin Wall acts as a symbol of the profound change in the state of being that will be necessary to effect a re-union.

Odysseus' war has removed his kingship and placed just such a wall between him, struggling out of the sea, and his homeland. The ceremony of planting his oar inland is a way of slowing down and re-acclimating himself. But how hard is it for him to do this, and beat sword into plowshare? How is the over-achieving, ever-alert, technologically-scheming Odysseus described by Loren Eiseley balanced with the Odysseus who returns to animal and human husbandry? It is precisely because, as Berry says in "From the Crest" (in *Clearing* 41), "the farm is an infinite form" that we have trouble believing in dramatic, short-term "Final Solutions" like

Odysseus' execution of suitors (who will, in time, re-appear with other names). Odysseus seems to be looking for a way out of the mortal common ground—where we are all born into the middle of history and language—that Western Civilization knows, in the title of one of anthropologist Mircea Eliade's books, as "the terror of history," where a misdeed can never be undone.

Yet Odysseus himself might turn to us and say, as Berry does in "Preserving Wildness" (*Home Economics* 138): "I would prefer to stay in the middle, not to avoid taking sides, but because I think the middle *is* a side, as well as the real location of the problem [of the relation of humanity to nature]." Similarly, Berry, in his point-by-point description of that harmony between nature and culture further along in the same essay, implies support for slower, more careful solutions when he says: "But I do not believe that it [harmony] can be achieved simply or easily or that it can ever be perfect, and I am certain that it can never be made, once and for all, but is the forever unfinished lifework of our species" (138-9). This is perhaps an admission that the middle in Western Civilization is not so much the gradual approach toward moderation (the real teaching of Epicurus?) as it is an equilibrium of violent extremes (captured in the misunderstanding of that same Epicurus as preacher of last-minute hedonism when he said, "Eat, drink and be merry, for tomorrow you die.").

Owen Barfield, I believe in *Poetry & Diction*, defined mythology as the "ghost of concrete meaning." This not only reminds us of the attempts to find the real Homer behind Odysseus, but helps us see that our concrete world of meanings can be interestingly haunted by the ghostly example of an Odysseus who is first warrior and wanderer, then husband and husbandman. In mythic terms, Odysseus offers us choices in a modern world often swinging wildly in its orientation between violent activism and pacifism, and between displacement and rootedness. Knowing that a crucial difference between the ancient world and our own is that we no longer condone slavery (in spite of its existence), it is ironic but fitting that Berry provides a further crucial antidote to Odysseus-the-violent-wanderer in his book on slavery, *The Hidden Wound*. Showing how Eumaios, the swineherd, becomes the opposite, but not contrary, of Odysseus, Berry offers what might be seen as a dream-like Jungian union as he explains:

Indeed, the two figures represent not only the opposite ends of the social scale, but two opposite, and mutually sustaining, kinds of faithfulness: *Odysseus' is the faithfulness which ventures and returns; Eumaios' that which remains and preserves* [my italics]. As the faithful servant Eumaios represents and speaks for the homeland; he is in charge of the ceremonies of hospitality and welcome. Odysseus' dependence, the idea that the king is incomplete in himself, is symbolized in that he first returns to his kingdom as the *guest of his servant* [Berry's italics]. If Odysseus may be said to represent the questing spirit, then Eumaios represents the order without which questing would be too costly or impossible; he is generous and ceremonious, as opposed to the suitors "who have no regard for anyone in their minds." (125-6)

Just as Eumaios accompanies Odysseus from the fields to the palace for the final episodes, and Odysseus settles in the fields at the very end, Wendell Berry's early and recent work are opposites that offer health through their union. Re-arranged, the titles of his books form—if not exactly a "continuous landscape of harmony"—a valuable spectrum of choice. From the "unsettling of America," the "hidden wound" of America's spiritual and geographic displacement moves toward the "openings" of "broken ground" and "unforeseen wilderness," through the "clearing" and "awakening" and "remembering" of "findings" to "the gift of good land," and a man standing by his word in the "country of marriage." In *Traveling at Home* (1988), Wendell Berry has come further home not to roost, but to begin again by treating wandering more tolerantly, at least when it is done on the land he chooses over and over. The title poem explains (also echoing Heraclitus):

> Even in a country you know by heart
> it's hard to go the same way twice.
> The life of the going changes.
> The chances change and make a new way.
> Any tree or stone or bird

can be the bud of a new direction. The
natural correction is to make intent
of accident. To get back before dark
is the art of going. (23)

The centripetal force that has been such an insistence in Berry's work,
drawing him closer to his farm and family and the example of the
hospitable Eumaios, is here balanced by the centrifugal urge to reach out
and explore the margins of his farm and region as if he were seeing it all
anew. In the beautifully-understated prose-piece in this collection, "A Walk
Down Camp Branch," Berry is again in the position of the returning
Odysseus, entering a landscape that is both familiar and mysterious. A
path, Berry tells us, is "the form and the symbol and the enactment of the
relationship [with the landscape]." If it is as "personal" and "comfortable"
as "old shoes," his familiar paths are, conversely, "seldom worn on the
ground." Rather, they are "habits of mind, directions and turns" (12). And
just as the ancient Greek "strophe" meant to "turn at the edge of the stage,"
so Berry is deflected by, and reflected in, the natural and agricultural margins of this land he is walking through. The unexpected bluebells found on
this walk are a discovery long prepared for. We recall the way the hawk
glides out of the walnut tree, across the margin and into the field Berry is
quietly mowing with his horses in "Getting Along With Nature" (in *Home
Economics* 13). Berry continues, there, to tell us that "the human eye itself
seems drawn to such margins," which are "biologically rich, the meeting of
two kinds of habitat."

The fuller meaning of the Odyssean myth is the paradox that, because of
the interdependence of polarities like content/form, nature/culture,
wilderness/city, war/peace, individual/society, and farm/nation, the
center of true community and communication is simultaneously at the
center and the margins of our experience. In the center of the black
half-circle of the Chinese yin/yang symbol is a point of white, just as there
is a point of black inside the parallel, co-existent, white semi-circle. Order
resides inside chaos, just as chaos sits within order. Heraclitus, the ancient
Greek Loren Eiseley uses above to remind us to "expect the unexpected,"
and whom J. Glenn Gray and Charles Olson conversely cite for his concern that we rediscover the familiar, is even better known for his dictum

that "the only thing that does not change is change itself." In our world defined by rapid changes, poet-scholar David Antin suggests that it is the past that is shifting most.

Yet the larger pattern of Wendell Berry's life reminds us we walk a delicate tightrope in the relentless present of often-dangerous choices. Our "common ground" now necessarily extends far afield of house and farm, as events like the nuclear catastrophe at Chernobyl or the pollution and carelessness causing the "greenhouse effect" keep demonstrating. When the ratio of American students studying abroad to foreign students studying in America remains at approximately one to eight, we are losing track of the world. Yet any careful traveler—who goes abroad not to replace his home, but rather to understand it—knows there is no McLuhan-like "instant global village." As Wendell Berry knows, nuclear weapons imply that for anyone's home to be safe, all people must have a home they can be proud of. Crucial world decisions must, therefore, begin at home, but be cautious both because we have, and have not, traveled. Should we, no matter what people say about the springs and workings of violence, answer as Barry Lopez, in *Of Wolves and Men*, tells us the Eskimos do when responding to anything said about wolves, with: "Maybe."? If so, we will be open to how we might balance our extremes as we follow a middle path already imagined, surveyed and lived by Homer, Epicurus, the great ecologists and ethnologists, and now Wendell Berry. In mapping the course all of us must follow between real contraries (whatever they turn out to be), Wendell Berry's healing oxymoron of "traveling at home"—so useful in revealing the extraordinary quality of daily life—is both an excellent point of origin and destination for the navigation of love.

Wendell Berry's
Husband to the World:
A Place on Earth

Jack Hicks

Farmer, professor, Wendell Berry has also had a prolific literary career since his first book, *Nathan Coulter*. He works in all forms—poetry, fiction, essays, drama—and with his most recent works of 1977, *Clearing* (poems) and *The Unsettling of America* (essays), has published twenty-two volumes.[1] From his artistic beginnings, he has shown an abiding interest in his Central Kentucky homelands. And like his fellow novelist of the land, Ernest J. Gaines, who sets his tales in the dust and bayous of rural Louisiana, Berry also tills a single native soil. His constant terrain has been the Upper Appalachian South, in the locale of Port William, Kentucky (a poetic imagining of his own Port Royal), spread across the rolling hills and cuts that drain into the Kentucky River. Berry's fictive families, mainly the distantly related Coulter and Feltner clans, are subsistence tobacco farmers and dwell in all three of his novels and much of his other work. Their stories are set mostly in the 1940's and 1950's, but they range as far back as the antebellum Simon Feltner (1784-1858) and span at least seven generations—actively and historically—in the novels.

"The earth is the genius of our life," Berry writes near the end of *A Place on Earth*, and from that earth and a sense of man's place in it, he has developed a moral vision of man in harmony with the land, a conservative Jeffersonian agrarian ideal rare and attractive to our times.[2] He has had help and pays frequent witness to his psychic kinsmen, to Jefferson and Thoreau and, more recently, to the Southern Agrarians of *I'll Take My Stand*, to William Carlos Williams and Gary Snyder.[3] Like that of his former Stanford classmates Gaines and Ken Kesey, Berry's work is centrally concerned with "the genius" of modern man in a specific geographical place, and his work speaks to those who yearn for a healing vision of the mingled lives of man and nature. He has gone back to the old ways, and the richness of his publication (*Esquire, Harper's, New York Times, Hudson Review* on one hand; on the other, *Mother Earth News, Organic Gardening and Farming*, Sierra Club Press) testifies to the broad appeal of his message.

The model of Berry's own life, recounted in the departures and returns to his family and calling and place in *The Long-Legged House* and in the recent poetry—especially in his restoration of the family Lanes Landing Farm in 1965—has nourished and been nourished by an extraordinary rich metaphor: man as husband, in the oldest sense of the word, having committed himself in multiple marriages to wife, family, farm, community, and finally to the cycle of great nature itself. This is the central stream of Wendell Berry's writing, his "country of marriage" (the title of a recent book of poems), the controlling pattern of his imagination, and it travels richly through the images, languages, tales of his work, just as the Kentucky River winds through the loamy tobacco lands that so possess his imagination.

Whether we speak of his polemics against the twin rapacities of strip mining and agribusiness (Berry is among the clearest contemporary ecological voices), the practical essays of *Organic Farm and Gardening*, the lyric celebrations of the feel of rain and wood and friendship, or his brooding tales of seven Port William generations, the informing vision is the same, a complex and coherent sense of man's need for a proper place on earth. His assumptions are unstated, at times in conflict, but in essence his view of man is as a distinctly flawed being fallen from natural wholeness. A ruined forest kingdom lies faintly in the background of Berry's work, idyllic and edenic, a prelapsarian, preagrarian world of unspoiled nature. A version of the destruction of that primal world is offered in a recent narrative poem, "The Kentucky River: July 1773."[4] This is the earliest historical moment in his Kentucky Valley saga and a reenactment of an ancient tragedy. Berry often links the voracious westering impulse in American history with the primal violation of nature, and here we see the first white explorers from Virginia, incredulous at the serene vitality of sacred Indian lands near Big Lick. While Berry does not stress the Christian element—indeed his work shows little sympathy with organized religion—his settlers are as near the garden as mortal man can ever return, held spell-bound, "for that upwelling / and abounding, unbidden by any / man, was powerful, bright, / and brief for men like these, / as a holy vision" (*Collected Poems* 221).

Young Sam Adams finds himself, entranced, in an unfrightened herd of grazing buffalo, a young player in an old scene, and fires his musket in their midst. His name suggests his role, and to Berry's mind, he is at once the first Adam falling from unity, the westering white man wasting nature in his path, a boy trumpeting the arrival of male sexuality. They are links in a chain of motifs related regularly in the work. The entire party is nearly trampled, and Berry painfully searches for motives, concluding: "He saw an amplitude / so far beyond his need / he could not imagine it, / and he could not let it be. / He shot" (222-3). Thus man, particularly the historical American white man, lives fragmented since his fall from harmony with nature, divided, condemned to "obscure or corrupt our understanding of any one of the basic unities" ("Discipline and Hope," in *A Continuous Harmony* 161). Berry's ideal husband is earthly man in his most noble state, doomed to separate consciousness, but in that single mind making a pact with the world, taking the vows of marriage, assuming the healing role of husband to wife, family, land. Farm, community, family, these are earthly compromises, the tropes in flesh and word and wood of mortal man, his ritual gestures to re-create whatever harmony he can. The farm itself is not a "natural" shape, but "an opening in a wilderness," a man-attended order, often an attempt by Berry's farmers to heal the geographical and historical scars of their wrong-headed ancestors (*A Continuous Harmony* 52).

The husband's literal and metaphoric role, as the language and substance of what Berry terms "the metaphor of atonement" suggest, is one of healing old wounds, of atoning for past violations, by the re-awakening in human consciousness of the sense of nature's "interlocking systems" (157), of the possibilities that human lives might share and thrive in the old organic dream ("at-one-ment," as a later gloss suggests). As we see later, this is an ideal, and ideal husbands, as Mat Feltner of *A Place on Earth* seems, are as rare as any ideal. Much of the tragedy and pathos in Berry's work originates in the failure—either willed or fated, conscious or unaware—of men to perceive a natural order or conduct their lives within it.

Pervasive though it is, the "metaphor of atonement" is most directly shaped in the essays of *A Continuous Harmony.* Here Berry writes of the sacred bonds between man and land, of the marriage of husband to his literal and mystic wife. In "Think Little," he involves Black Elk, holy seer of the Oglala Sioux, and his visions of the interconnectedness of all life: "I saw that the sacred hoop of my people was one of many hoops that made a circle, wide as daylight and as starlight, and in the circle grew the mighty flowering tree to shelter all the children of one mother and father. And I saw that it was holy" (*A Continuous Harmony* 85). "Discipline and Hope," his most ambitious essay, calls several witnesses: Inca historian John Collier notes the tribal unit, the *ayllu,* is based in "not merely its people and not merely the land, but people and land wedded through a mystical bond"; and Rhodesian Tangwena Chief Rekayi calmly refuses to cede ancestral land to whites, explaining, "I am married to this land. I was put here by God." (102)

Sioux, Inca, Tangwena: these are tribal cultures, "primitive" images of noble pasts. Berry chases the thread closer, to Thomas Jefferson, whom he quotes as describing farmers as "tied to their country, and wedded to its liberty and interests, by the most lasting bonds." It is finally in "Discipline and Hope," against this historical chorus, that he most clearly shapes his moral and literary vision:

> Living in our speech, though no longer in our consciousness, is an ancient system of analogies that clarifies a series of mutually defining and sustaining unities: of farmer and field, of husband and wife, of the world and God. . . . A man planting a crop is like a man making love to his wife and vice versa: . . . . he is like a plant in a field waiting for rain. . . . All the essential relationships are comprehended in this metaphor. A farmer's relation to his land is the basic and central connection in the relation of humanity to the creation; the agricultural relation *stands for* the larger relation. Similarly, marriage is the basic and central community tie; it begins and stands for the relation we have to family and to the larger circles of human association.

> And these relationships to the creation and to the human community are in turn basic to, and may stand for, our relationship to God—or to the sustaining mysteries and powers of the creation. . . . If the metaphor of atonement is alive in [a man's] consciousness, he will see that he should love and care for his land as for his wife, that his relation to his place in the world is as solemn and demanding, and as blessed, as marriage; and he will see that he should respect his marriage as he respects the mysteries and transcendent powers—that is, as a sacrament. Or—to move in the opposite direction through the changes of the metaphor—in order to care properly for his land he will see that he must emulate the Creator; to learn to use and preserve the open fields . . . he must study and follow natural process; he must understand the *husbanding* that, in nature, always accompanies providing. (159-161)

My interest here is in the continuity of Berry's vision, and particularly in how the image of the exemplary husband—in his ideal and lesser aspects—is refracted in his novels, most especially, in the fullest and most satisfying fiction to date, *A Place on Earth*.

The world of Port William is male-dominated, and the first depiction of it is in *Nathan Coulter*, a spare *bildungsroman* made up of the protagonist's episodic recollections of his formative years, roughly to age fourteen. The lessons of manhood and the instructions of husbandry are hard-learned and seldom gentle. In the figure of young Nathan, Berry depicts an *apprentice-husband*, one who will discover the many stern vocations of farm marriage. Filtered as it is, back through a youthful first-person consciousness, the novel shows little of the rich verdure of history that characterizes Wendell Berry's best work, few of the intertwinings of character—their lives and pasts that suggest the ripe weight of past on present.

Young Nathan's stark recollections are truly of a ruined kingdom, for what he remembers are not so much the "sacred hoops" of man and wife, family, the worlds of the fields and the woods. His discoveries are not of what is, but what is lacking. From his earliest sense of separate consciouusness ("I'm Nathan Coulter. It seemed strange."), his memories are suffused with awkwardness and alienation and finally multiple loss of innocence, of parents and siblings, of community (*Nathan Coulter* 18). The emphasis is on the rending of the organic fabric, and this apprentice sees many failures of the dream of harmony, a long sequence of disrupted relationships between husbands and the natural world.

As in much of Berry's work, the major thematic interest is in death, in Nathan's gradual awareness of it, in how one deals with it or does not, and death is omnipresent: in the natural deaths of fish and game that he and his mentor, Uncle Burley, harvest in the dramatic background; in the death of his own pained childhood; in the more metaphoric deaths of the body of the family and his father's spirit.

Nathan cannot accept the role of husband to this damaged world (although he has returned five years later in *A Place on Earth*), and as he leaves near the end of the novel, he takes a last look backward to see a mirroring of several deaths: "I could see them all through the window, sitting with Daddy by Grandpa's coffin, keeping their separate silences, their faces half shadow in the dim light" (203).

Ninety-two year old Jack Beechum, central figure of *The Memory of Old Jack*, is the master to the youth's apprenticeship, a declining husband of the old ways, one whose death raises "the possibility that men of his kind are a race doomed to extinction" (*The Memory of Old Jack* 215). The "memory" of the title is doubly significant. First, the novel is indeed a memory, an elegy and a requiem for the oaklike old man whose final earthly day in September, 1952, is the fictional present. For the men working in the tobacco shed three months later—the Feltners and Coulters and Penns and Catletts—he has indeed been "a monument . . . a public statue" (3-4), an emblem of the husband and his legacy. The novel closes on their agreement that death can end a life but cannot cancel it, that the remembered substance of Old Jack Beechum will be as rich as his physical presence, that "the like of him will not soon live again in this world, and they will not forget him" (223).

It is also "memory" in a second sense, for Beechum's last day is a series of journeys back into memories of the past, interlaced with those of friends and relatives in Port William. The main substance of the novel is precisely this mixture of reminiscence and reflection, of the marbled history of the aged husband, his work and town and land and tragic marriage. The growth of nascent consciousness kindles our interest in the future of the protagonist; the lying-down of old age cants our attentions back to an earlier time. Youth and old age, *Nathan Coulter* and *The Memory of Old Jack* are end pieces, and between the two stands Wendell Berry's most developed image of husbandry, *A Place on Earth*.

The emphasis in *A Place on Earth* is on the mature husband, and as the title and recurrent language of the novel suggest, on his *place* within the organic cycles of nature. The pattern here, both implicit and explicit, is the seasonal cycle of animal and vegetal life—of sowing, germination, fruition, death, decay—and Berry develops the life of his central character, Mat Feltner, and the various marriages and families and farms of Port William, and of the larger social worlds beyond, in terms of how they do or do not partake of these natural cycles.

Feltner is the ideal husband to the world, a striving upward in the flesh, back toward unity with the natural world. He is defined, dramatically, by his struggle with the meaning of his son Virgil's death, and—more statically—by exemplary images and tales of lesser men around him. They take many shapes, as men like Simon Crop, who because of their fate and weakness make a more tenuous pact with woman and farm. Or they are Berry's pathetic or tragic cases, the flawed and failed husbands—like Jarrett Coulter or Jack Beechum—who have failed to find the continuities they sought. Or they are bachelors, like Jayber Crow, Burley Coulter and Ernest Finley, who have refused or been refused the varied healing roles of the husband.

From the time the novel opens, the setting—the interrelations of weather and season and place—is not merely a backdrop but an active presence. "The seed bins are empty," we start, and it is here that the arcs of seasonal growth and fictional development start: in stasis and darkness ("time as a succession of nights"), as a drear late winter rain, "the very presence and noise of emptiness," drums on the tin roof overhead (*A Place on Earth* 3). It is early March, 1945, and four men (Mat Feltner, Frank Lathrop, Jack Beechum, Burley Coulter) play a desultory game of rummy "expectant of sound . . . anticipating an arrival," waiting for the stalled coming of the planting season. "They're waiting," we note, "for the war to be over, for whatever resumption of continuities and certainties will take place at the end of it" (13). By the close of the novel in late autumn, 1945, the seasons will have turned again. The attended or unattended lives of forest and croplands, of livestock and orchards, of men and women and their families, will also have turned within that cycle, some with it, for good, some against it for tragic ends. And the world of Port William and the life of the husband will return to the rain and darkness from which they issued, with a renewed sense of rest in winter.

The opening anxious gloom is appropriate psychic weather for Mat and Margaret Feltner, for they have had no word from their son, at war in Europe. The letter arrives, confirming Virgil "missing in action," and much of the body of the novel is taken up with the tensions and meanings of his loss, both to the Feltners and to his pregnant wife, Hannah, who lives with them. Though Virgil's death seems unnatural set against the coming spring, it is not unusual at this stage in the life of Port William, for a recurring motif is the loss of the young to battle and catastrophe. Tom Coulter and Virgil die in Europe. Nathan Coulter leaves early in the action, and Jasper Lathrop and Billy Gibbs also serve. Young Annie Crop will be swept away later in a violent spring flash flood. It is as if the future of the town, its young life, is being amputated. Their losses are wounds to the social body, and Berry continues that image in a rich pattern of detail throughout the novel. The languages of healing and scarring prevail; farmers wound and scar their land and wives in ignorance; whole lives (like Ernest Finley's) are weak healings over mortal injury; Virgil's loss is a trauma to the social body and the psychic life of the husband. Set against the coming greenness, all such destructions are difficult to reconcile, seem almost moral violations to the natural order.[5]

Mat tries to distract himself, but the loss of his only son threatens his entire life. He has lost "a sense of continuity," we are told, and he reaches out for "life, more purely than he ever conceived it before—his son's life and his own, restored, healed, made whole" (331). Virgil's death seems to cancel his own being, and even the trees and buildings are totemic, ghostly "monuments to a failed past" (25).

As Mat Feltner fingers the ragged wound of Virgil's death, his mind loops back through his own past. Again Berry works in cycles, here to most basically suggest the historical roots of the husband's past and to depict his many intertwining marriages. The richness of *A Place on Earth* is an accumulation of such retrogressions into individual pasts (just as the soil lives as a present corpus of past leaves and bodies), and in Mat's chapter, Berry underscores the most dominant concerns of the husband's life: work, history, marriage itself.

Mat remembers himself as a boy in the country, romping with friends "wild as foxes," and, as we are reminded in a long historical sketch, Port William was also young and unshaped, possessing "a certain wildness about it" (147). For a time, he lives "free of his life" but come to serve a kind of "apprentice manhood," first in daredevil play in the river bottoms, and later, in reality, at age fourteen, when his father introduces him to the sweat of the field: "I want you to learn what work is, how it's done, and how a man makes himself able to do it. If you don't learn that as a boy when you've got energy enough . . . you'll never learn it as a man" (156).

So Mat comes to tobacco farming as a youth; and, through the punishing work—from the tilth of the black soil breaking open under the plow, to the cutting and sorting of the winey burley into hands and sticks, to the final discing of the field—he becomes a man. Work is important in Berry's world, testifying to a man's relationship to nature; ideally, as exhausting as it is, the husband's labor is an entering into the rhythms and harmonies of natural growth. Work is a song, attended by music in these novels, a poetic celebration of the escape from the solitary self to temporary wholeness, an action by which he nourishes and is nourished by his wife, the land. So Mat learns to value the sweat shed by men stooping in rows and to ease his labor in work chants ("Hundred dollars waiting on a dime. / Show it to me boys. / Make me know it" [156]).

Mat is significantly most fulfilled in the literal work of plant and animal husbandry. He takes his deepest pleasures among live-stock and orchards, and we see him often in barns, lower pens and fruit fields. Birthing animals, his life takes shape before him. He "hungers for the births and lives of his animals," Berry writes, "he's more at peace with himself than he is at any other time" (115). Delivering lambs, he experiences a Brueghelesque ecstasy; "The life of things, standing up in a lamb or a plant, is his vision and his justification and his blessing" (117). The prose carries the same lyric intensity in depicting him among the fruit trees. Here again, he is most alive in husbandry, on a pruning ladder surrounded by "delicately colored shoots of last year's new growth. Loving their color and shape and feel, the whiplike life of them." And Berry concludes, "His working with these trees has always been one of the freest and happiest of his labors" (266).

So work is a kind of kinetic prayer, a witnessing and affirming of man's active place in the natural world, and it is also a means by which history and character are revealed in *A Place on Earth.* Mat Feltner is the moral norm, and approaches the ideal husband (as steward) in his ability to work within nature and within his own farming group—Burley Coulter, Joe Banion, Big Ellis, and neighbor Elton Penn, Old Jack's "adopted" heir—share, in different styles, his balance. The labor of man is a main theme throughout the novel, and other characters and families are tested—and often found wanting—by their relationships to work. There are the slothful, like the derelict bootlegger Whacker Spradlin, for whom narrative scorn undercuts sympathy. A career drunk, he is the last fizzling of Hoss Spradlin, a hard but misguided worker. His father devours the world, would "replace a broken window with a sheet of tin, or drive a tack with an axe." Finally, his fate " was to be a user of land and work animals and tools that other men had worn out" (28). Disordered and numbly refusing all work (his customers help themselves), Whacker represents a further decline, the swing of the pendulum from his father's manic energy. Roger Merchant, Feltner's indolent cousin, is also a severed thread, a lazy caricature of the "gentleman farmer." Like Hoss Spradlin, his father "lived on his land like a blight on it," as if "an angel had appeared to him, saying: 'There it is. Use it up. Get all you can out of it'" (178). Here, too, the son is an image of familial and personal decline.

The Spradlin and Merchant clans are dying, and the scions in each case are only sons, shrivelled images of historical deterioration, characterized mainly in their refusal or inability to do fruitful work. There is also the opposite imbalance, seen most vividly in Jarrett Coulter. Mat's contemporary and Nathan's father, he is an instance of increasing isolation and moral disorder. Jarrett Coulter is a stern and loveless patriarch in *Nathan Coulter,* presiding over a household that dies under his touch. His wife and father pass, and he drives his sons from his house and is left alone, finally, in a mutated relationship to his land and labor. He is one of Berry's ruined husbands, seized in a cancerous, abstract obsession with his land. A generation older in *A Place on Earth,* Jarrett Coulter's decline is more pronounced, and he again represents the masculine impulse to shape and order gone wild. His life is driven by a grim energy to harness the natural world, and his work is a kind of race, as "He bears down on a crop as a runner bears down on a tape." His dream is an exaggerated reverie of "perfect order and perfect weather," and to this unnatural end, his labor is relentless, has "created failures of friendships between him and his sons, and him and his neighbors, and has carried him past them—into a silence that he has made his calling and his answer" (528).

Part I, Chapter 3, devoted to Mat's past, depicts a second concern of the husband—history—and again, the element is active in many lives in the novel. If nature reels in continuing cycles, so too does the present life of a man or a family or a town from the past. History is a kind of root stock in *A Place on Earth*, and the many pasts of people and places give branch to and enrich the narrative present of the novel. Summoned directly in the strong narrative voice, or as family apocrypha over ham and biscuits at the supper table, or as town gossip in Jayber Crow's barber shop or Frank Lathrop's store, the multiple histories accumulate and serve to gloss the positive instance of Mat Feltner's life.

Child, adolescent, adult, Mat's own personal and family history has been a preparation for his life as a mature husband. What emerges from the pattern of his life—Berry emphasizes this—is that he finally *elects* his role, takes vows of marriage to his wife and place and people. Further, he was historically prepared for it, perhaps even *fated* for it, so that he does indeed finally "choose what he'd been destined to choose" (173).

And here again, the tendrils of history and fate extend through many lives. The narrative line is deflected regularly from the season of 1945, taking us into the histories of the major male characters—Jarrett and Burley Coulter, Ernest Finley, Jayber Crow, Gideon Crop. If Mat's life is a vital harmony, a balance of past and present, fate and free choice, personal duty and family obligation, there is also an attendant strain of imbalance, of historical misfortune and tragedy. Fate can write one's doom, or one can be driven by a false sense of historical imperative. Each case is symptomatic, like bad work, of unnaturalness, disorder. One of the earliest of the Feltner clan, former slavetrader and Confederate "officer" Jefferson Feltner is a case of historical myopia, another instance of the masculine need to order run unchecked. After the War, he is obsessed with "honor" and "loss of past," becomes a zealot who fights constantly to defend a misvision of person and family. His life is a martial dance, an extended, ruthless vignette of the dangers of historical illusion, and he is "the servant and instrument, and finally the victim, of his history" (152). More pitifully, Roger Merchant languishes in a besotted fantasy, "an uncritical devotion to what he called his family tradition" (179). He reaches a dead end, bachelor son of a failed and ravenous husband, alone and unwed to woman, soil or people, a man who "has built nothing, added nothing, repaired nothing" (182). And his illusions of his scruffy father "as a cultivated and enlightened gentleman farmer," and his own latter years of "a little light fawming" are the solipsisms of the bottle, as passive a historical fantasy as Jefferson Feltner's were active, but no less destructive.

The long and tragic story of Ernest Finley's life and suicide is perhaps the most moving tale in *A Place on Earth* and drives home the lesson that history and fate play active roles in human life. A local carpenter, Finley is a meticulous craftsman, a quiet, respected friend and worker. While his suicide first seems shocking and aberrant, reflection suggests that it has been well-prepared, and his self-destructive act seems finally almost unavoidable. Also one of Wendell Berry's bachelors, Finley returns to Port William after World War I, apparently to pick up his life in the community. But his ties have been irremediably severed. His parents dead, his family house and lands dispersed, Ernest has also been war-crippled; he is shown to be a man historically and personally wounded, fated to a tragic end. He is a physical and psychic cripple, described recurringly in the language of scars and scarring. His body is a metaphysical damage report, "fragmented bones and tendons were spliced back together and packaged in scar tissue" (47); his nickname, "Shamble," is "placed on his life like a scar, the healing of a wound and its betrayal" (51). Even his apparent virtues, serenity and patience, are finally delusive surfaces, keloids like his shop, "a walling-in of his desire" (52). His life is another dead end.

Following the flash flood that devastates the Crop household, sweeping Annie away (and Gideon in a crazed search for her), Ernest works neighborly to repair damaged outbuildings. Berry lingers over his shy, gradual attachment to Ida, his unwitting attempt to deny his history and fate. Gideon writes that he is returning, and the strange house of Ernest's need collapses around him, "as if sunk into the blinding whiteness of Gideon's letter" (462). His aberrant "marriage" to Ida has been historically and socially unnatural, and his suicide—at first shocking—seems finally a kind of healing. Death is a part of the natural process—the end and the beginning, this is to be Mat's lesson—and Ernest's end is a grim picture of the death of a crippled line, the healing return of blood to the natural earth. Mat Feltner finds him in a workshop corner, dead on his knees, both wrists deeply and carefully cut, his blood drained through a newly-sawed hole in the floorboards.

Like Ernest, whose history seems to refuse him the easings of husbandry, even life itself, many of Berry's men are widowed or unwed. This is no paradise of bachelors: bitter Jarrett Coulter and the old chief Jack Beechum are widowers; Roger Merchant, Burley Coulter, Jayber Crow, and Ernest Finley, for all their differences, have refused or been refused the vows of husband and father. From Mat's pained broodings, he is eased as he turns to this third consideration, marriage. A man's life is a statement, and marriage and its human condition are ideally a statement in flesh of the multiple vows of the husband. Like the lives of man and town, his married life has grown from childhood to maturity. He and Margaret Feltner are childhood friends, and their long courtship is a complex process, often painful, of his learning to accept her as wife and partner. His return to Port William after college and travel is a multiple acceptance, of "his life before him: his marriage, his place, his work" (173).

Throughout the novel, the emphasis on marriage, on the joining of male and female, is decidedly on the faces of friendship, partnership, parenting. Berry draws few scenes of sexual love or passion, indeed sexuality—especially male sexuality—often threatens marital harmony. Mat's own incipient adolescent sexuality, for example, threatens his relationship with Margaret until he masters it, and "their estrangement slowly healed" (164). And the protagonist's coltish discovery of male energy in *Nathan Coulter* is devastating: his first sexual experience with Mrs. Mandy Loyd is a re-enactment of man's primal violation of natural order, ruining the Loyd marriage, disrupting his family, nearly costing him his life.

Berry's farm marriages are more characterized by quiet respect, support, endurance, than by passion, intensity, or personal encounter. Marriage is distinctly man-made, "a practical curcumstance," he writes in "Discipline and Hope," as he emphasizes the homespun aspect, "it must make a household, it must make a place for itself in the world and the community" (*A

Continuous Harmony 103). When his wives are depicted as sexual beings, it is most often as a fruitful presence, as an embodiment of the feminine principle, the less-treated but fully complementary partner to the will to husband. The pregnant Hannah, for an instance, continues life just as the death of her young husband threatens that continuity. Despondent in his loss, Mat finds solace in her presence. Big with child, she is shown among livestock and flowering orchards, healing the break, carrying and nourishing life just as she bears a spray of peach boughs, "the graceful curving and slendering of them weighted and knobbed with buds" (267).

Like work, marriage is a rising up, ideally a merging of the solitary selves, an act of healing and partial reconciliation with nature. Though the Feltner marriage is a model, many others are less successful. Apparently doomed to tenant farm Roger Merchant's land and never work their own, Ida and Gideon Crop live with fewer hopes in a weaker bond. Driven by a sense of futility, Gideon vents his despair in drinking bouts in fishing camps. She waits doggedly for him, continuing their work, resigned: "It doesn't surprise her that her marriage has failed to be an idyl of romance; she never expected it would be" (190). The marriage made by local "character" Uncle Stanley Gibb and "Miss Pauline" is a strained comedy. Sexton of the church and the town gravedigger, Uncle Stanley is a constant, garrulous witness to an empty house "where they live like strangers who happen to have rooms in the same hotel." He and his "Christian" wife share "a grim watchful armistice, likely to break into hostilities any minute" (95).

The central tragedy of Jack Beechum's life, shown in greater detail in *The Memory of Old Jack* is, likewise, his mismade marriage to Ruth Lightwood. Successful as a husband to his land and town, he fails in marriage. He and Ruth are very different people, and marriage proves "the great disaster of both their lives" (*The Memory of Old Jack* 57). Strongly attracted to each other, they mislead themselves in illusion, and even their passions finally separate them, as "They lay beside each other in solitude, as rigid and open-eyed as effigies" (59). Turning to a secret love affair with the widow Rose McGinnis, Jack is for a time delighted, but love needs the shape of a marriage to flourish in this world, and it is finally "as though he bore for these two women the two halves of an irreparably divided love. With Ruth his work led to no good love. With Rose, his love led to no work" (143). Old Jack's unlucky story lingers in the mind of Port William, "troubling and consoling the night watches of lonely husbands and wives like a phrase from a forgotten song" (132).

The disrupted marriage begun by Virgil and Hannah Feltner has been quite the opposite, as clear-eyed and strong as there is in Berry's world, but it remains, ironically, for a bachelor, barber Jayber Crow, to give most eloquent voice to the husband's ideal state. He is a kind of "bachelor-witness" to the husband's life, monkishly eschewing marriage to celebrate it most intensely in higher form. In vow-like cadences, Jayber imagines it as "a kind of last-ditch holy of holies: the possibility that two people might care for each other and know each other better than enemies, and better than strangers, and better than accidentally by happening to be alive at the same time in the same town; and that, with a man and a woman, this caring and knowing might be made by intention, and in the consciousness of all it is, and all it might be, and of all that threatens it" (96-7). Crow's true name is Jonah, and he is a real survivor of his own trials, imagining in his cell above the shop, Port William as radiant:

> A kind of Heavenly City, in which each house would be built
> in a marriage and around it, and all houses would be bound to-
> gether in friendships, and friendliness would move and join a-
> mong them like an open street. (97)

History, work, marriage, these are the major chords of Mat Feltner's life in his earthly city, and they resonate throughout *A Place on Earth*. Yet the husband's whole received and elected life is threatened by his son's death. Mat's chapter closes on the pain and darkness of its origin, and when he returns to earth, he faces and surpasses his crisis. The husband's task is to re-discover man's own mortal place, to yield his pride before a greater scheme, and to this end, he is instructed by his mystic and literal wives. Margaret speaks to him of endurance and acceptance of their mutual state: "From the day he was born I knew he would die. . . . I knew so well that he would die that, when he did. . . . I was familiar with the pain. I'd had it in me all his life." She continues, confronting the central issue: "I don't believe that when his death is subtracted from his life, it leaves nothing." Mat is eased and renewed, her words falling on him "like light . . . He feels himself rinsed and wrung, mad fit" (451).

The husband is made ready for a second piece of advice, from his mystic wife, the soil. It is offered through Jack Beechum as he and Mat sit ritually through the night with Ernest Finley's body. Beechum once also lost his only son, and this is a tribal message from an ancient head to his successor, returning his attention to his roots in the earth:

> The old man spoke of the names and landmarks and happenings of a time before Mat's birth, and Mat listened, his mind drawn back before its own beginning, held and quieted by the vision of another time, and by a sense of the quiet continuance of the land, the place, through all that has happened on it and to it—its troubling history of a little cherishing and much abuse. For as always it was finally the land that they spoke of, fascinated as they've been all their lives by what has happened to it, their own ties to it, the wife of their race, more lovely and bountiful and kind than they have usually deserved, more severe and demanding than they have often been able to bear. (499)

Mat is comforted at the end, mainly by his re-discovery—for it is the husband's duty to find and find again such threads—of the process of renewal in nature. Mortal life is a compromise, and the splintered figures of man's stay, his atonement, are temporary. Sons, family, marriage, town: they will surely die (and Nathan will return from war, Hannah's child be born, a new crop taken in, and younger husbands will step forward). Berry's husband to the world comes through with a richer, reconciling sense of the natural cycle. It is an old message, that "For every thing there is a season," as the Preacher teaches in Ecclesiastes, and in Mat's daybook, he finally records coming to "a vision of this land here. . . . underlying all the changes that come upon it and pass over it, all the lives that in their seasons and times rise on it to grow, bloom, make seed, die, and descend again into it. I've learned the patterns its lives make, from its men to its weeds, and I have grown ever less willing to set myself against any of them" (544).

"He must look to the woods," Wendell Berry advises us of the proper husband, and Mat Feltner does just that (*A Continuous Harmony* 161). Walking his land, Mat is surprised to find a stand of trees overgrowing ruined tobacco plots, a healing of the "virgin wealth" his ancestors have spent. He sits down as leaves fall and night advances, and "seems to come deeper into the presence of the place," becomes "part of a design, where death can only give into life." No longer struggling, he accepts his condition, that "the order he has made and kept in [those clearings] will be overthrown, and the effortless order of wilderness will return to them" (550). He is eased, he is returning, once again, to his place on earth.

NOTES

1 This includes publications by major American houses and all significant editions by small presses. Chronologically, the books of poetry are: *November twenty six, nineteen hundred sixty three* (New York, 1964); *The Broken Ground* (New York, 1966); *Openings* (New York, 1968); *Findings* (Omaha, Ne., 1969); *Farming: A Hand Book* (New York, 1970); *The Country of Marriage* (New York, 1973); *An Eastward Look* (Berkeley, Ca., 1974); *Horses* (Monterey, Ky., 1975); *To What Listens* (Crete, Ne., 1975); *Sayings and Doings* (Lexington, Ky., 1975); *The Kentucky River: Two Poems* (Monterey, Ky., 1976); *Three Memorial Poems* (Berkeley, Ca., 1977); and *Clearing* (New York, 1977). Collections of essays are: *The Rise* (Lexington, Ky., 1968); *The Long-Legged House* (New York, 1969); *The Hidden Wound* (Boston, 1970); *The Unforeseen Wilderness* (Lexington, Ky., 1971); *A Continuous Harmony* (New York, 1972); and *The Unsettling of America* (San Francisco, 1977). His three novels are: *Nathan Coulter* (Boston, 1960); *A Place on Earth* (New York, 1967); and *The Memory of Old Jack* (New York, 1974) All further references are to these editions.

2 *A Place on Earth*, p.544.

3 See especially the essays "A Secular Pilgrimage," "A Homage to Dr. Williams," and "Discipline and Hope" in *A Continuous Harmony*.

4 "The Kentucky River: July 1773", in *The Kentucky River: Two Poems* [Reprinted as "July 1773" in *Collected Poems*, pp. 217-244]. Subsequent references are parenthetical in the text.

5 The imagery is alive throughout Berry's work. The controlling metaphor of the essays in *The Hidden Wound*, for example, is the legacy of American racism as an ancient, unhealed injury.

Thoreau and Wendell Berry: Bachelor and Husband of Nature

Herman Nibbelink

Wendell Berry's agrarian fiction, poetry, and essays—twenty-eight volumes thus far—counter the drift of American literature away from a consideration of farming as husbandry. Berry claims dignity for the farmer and a cultural and ecological necessity for agriculture as distinguished from agribusiness. His respect for nature and his understanding of its implications for culture have reminded readers of Thoreau; and in an excellent study of Berry's novel, *A Place on Earth,* Jack Hicks proposes that Thoreau is one of Berry's "psychic kinsmen."[1] It is a kinship that deserves further definition, for Thoreau was squeamish about husbandry and full of cranky complaints about farmers. "As for farming," he once wrote, "I am convinced that my genius dates from an older era than the agricultural. . . . What have I to do with plows?"[2]

Berry is the first to remind us of his own high regard for Thoreau. "Man cannot be independent of nature," he says in an early essay. "In one way or another he must live in relation to it, and there are only two alternatives: the way of the frontiersman, whose response to nature was to dominate it . . . or the way of Thoreau, who went to the natural places to become quiet in them, to learn from them, to be restored by them" (*The Long-Legged House* 41-42). Elsewhere, Berry has placed Thoreau in company with Marvell and Wordsworth (*A Continuous Harmony* 4), Homer and Dante (*A Continuous*

Harmony 64), and thus called him "a man of the rarest genius" (*Recollected Essays* 179). Much as Thoreau asserted his independent view of nature against both those who would destroy and those who would cheapen it ("the mealy-mouthed . . . lover of nature" [*A Week on the Concord and Merrimack Rivers* 109]), so Berry's independent cast of mind separates him from an urbanity removed from nature, from agribusiness, and from any mealy mouths among the current voices calling us back to nature. The poem that serves as prologue in *Clearing* may illustrate:

> My fields and walls are aching
> in my shoulders. My subjects are my objects:
> house, barn, beast, hill and tree.
> Reader, make no mistake. The meanings
> of these must balance against their weight.[3]

It is *Clearing*, a seven-part poetic account of the Berry family's settlement on Lanes Landing Farm in Henry County, Kentucky, that most nearly approximates Thoreau's *Walden*. Berry's essays frequently recall Thoreau by quotation and acknowledgement, as well as in echoes of Thoreau's thought and style; but *Clearing* offers "a simple and sincere account"—as disarmingly complex as Thoreau's—of the decision "to live deliberately" where one might "front only the essential facts of life, and see . . . what it had to teach."[4] A reading of *Clearing* with *Walden* in mind, especially the bean-field chapter, may demonstrate the affinity of these writers and identify their kinship while it distinguishes their views about the place of agriculture in the relationship of nature and culture.

The farmer is the first of his myopic neighbors Thoreau characterizes in *Walden*:

> I see young men, my townsmen, whose misfortune it is to have
> inherited farms, houses, barns, cattle, and farming tools. . . .
> How many a poor immortal soul have I met well nigh crushed
> and smothered under its load, creeping down the road of life,
> pushing before it a barn seventy-five feet by forty, its Augean
> stables never cleansed, and one hundred acres of land, tillage,
> mowing, pasture, and wood-lot . . .

> But men labor under a mistake. The better part of the man
> is soon ploughed into the soil for compost.

Indeed, one of the chief antagonists in *Walden* is the incipient agribusiness-man. "I respect not his labors," Thoreau says, "his farm where everything has its price, who would carry the landscape, who would carry his God, to market, if he could get anything for him" (196). Berry agrees with Thoreau about the cultural disease carried as the materialist burden; but his Jeffersonian vision of a nation of small farmers, caring about their land and one another, differs radically from Thoreau's view of agriculture even while it recalls a Thoreau-like respect for nature. "As many as possible should share in the ownership of the land," Berry says, "and thus be bound to it by economic interest, by the investment of love and work, by family loyalty, by memory and tradition." He asserts that this "old idea is still full of promise. It is potent with healing and with health" (*The Unsettling of America* 13-14). Thoreau begrudgingly acknowledges only a still older version of the idea in *Walden* and immediately qualifies it: "Ancient poetry and mythology suggest, at least, that husbandry was once a sacred art; but it is pursued with irreverent haste and heedlessness by us, our object being to have large farms and large crops merely" (165). Thoreau made no attempt to revive the sacred art, not even in his bean field.

"He chose, wisely, no doubt, for himself, to be the bachelor of thought and Nature," Emerson said of Thoreau in his famous biographical sketch. This judgement, applied to Thoreau's short-lived affair with his beans, may account for much of the ironic, self-deprecating humor mixed into the pungent social criticism and often-noticed transcendental poetics of this chapter of *Walden*. "What was the meaning of this so steady and self-respecting, this small Herculean labor, I knew not," Thoreau says. "I came to love my rows, my beans, though so many more than I wanted. They attached me to the earth, and so I got strength like Antaeus. But why should I raise them? Only Heaven knows" (155). A sprinkling of clichés and allusions to mythology flavors the blend of ironic puzzlement and a seemingly embarrased, though blunt, confession of his attraction to the acts of husbandry. With "little aid from . . . improved implements of husbandry," Thoreau says, he "became much more intimate" with his beans; but a blush appears on the face of his prose with his awareness of how others must see him: "A very *agricola laboriosus* was I to travellers bound . . . to nobody knows where" (157). He might resemble "the home-staying, laborious native of the soil," but he hastens to explain that his field "was, as it were, the connecting link between wild and cultivated fields . . . a half-cultivated field. They were beans cheerfully returning to their wild and primitive state that I cultivated, and my hoe played the *Ranz des Vaches* for them" (158). His concluding remarks about the personal values of the experience are hardly satisfying:

> Those summer days . . . I thus, with the other farmers of New England, devoted to husbandry. Not that I wanted beans to eat, for I am by nature a Pythagorean, so far as beans are concerned, whether they mean porridge or voting, and exchanged them for rice; but, perchance, as some must work in fields if only for the sake of tropes and expression, to serve a parable-maker one day. It was on the whole a rare amusement, which, continued too long, might have become a dissipation. Though I gave them no manure, and did not hoe them all once, I hoed them unusually well as far as I went. (162)

The chapter continues with the familiar monetary account of the bean crop and a little practical advice about raising beans—both laden with implied social criticism—and a moral lesson about "the seeds of . . . virtues" (164). Then Thoreau moves onto the firmer ground of his attack on materialism. "By avarice and selfishness," he says, "and a groveling habit, from which none of us is free, of regarding the soil as property, or the means of acquiring property chiefly, the landscape is deformed, husbandry is degraded with us, and the farmer leads the meanest of lives" (165). But he does not suggest that husbandry might be upgraded; instead, this once sacred art which briefly offered him a labor of love became at last "a rare amusement" from which it was necessary to extricate himself lest it "become a dissipation." Neither does Thoreau draw from the experience a lesson his own typical analogies might lead us to expect—that his neglect to fertilize his bean field might be related to the reason why "the seeds [of virtue] which I planted . . . did not come up" (164).

In general, Thoreau's bean field account is consistent with the ironic

pattern—the interplay between attraction (or involvement) and detach-
ment—that pervades *Walden.* However, in the light of Emerson's remark
about the extent of his bachelorhood, we may see what in particular this
parable-maker was up to in his bean field and why he brags "as lustily as
Chanticleer" one moment and, by allusion and irony, diverts our attention
from embarrassment in the next. The parable of the bean field is that of a
bachelor's dalliance, an experience that confirms his manhood and presumably authorizes him to speak out against permanent conjugal relationships. His love is qualified by irony, his attraction moderated by detach-
ment; remaining sensitive to the appeal of nature, he has resolved to be its
appreciative observer, having concluded that a closer relationship would be
degrading.

It is not sensuality that troubles Thoreau here; it is commitment, marriage. "The Indian's intercourse with Nature is at least such as admits of
the greatest independence of each," he said in the book written while he
lived at Walden Pond. "If he is somewhat of a stranger in her midst, the
gardener is too much of a familiar. There is something vulgar and foul in
the latter's closeness to his mistress" (*A Week on the Concord and Merrimack Rivers* 56). It is no wonder, then, that Thoreau worried over his right "to oust
johnswort and the rest" (*Walden* 155) of the weeds from his bean patch.
That he discreetly sowed beans instead of wild oats brought his affair
uncomfortably close to matrimony.

Justly concerned about the destructiveness of commercial farming and
land development, Thoreau is no less concerned about the loss of individual freedom resulting from commitment to the soil. "As long as possible,"
he says, "live free and uncommitted. It makes but little difference whether
you are committed to a farm or the county jail" (84). Enslavement of the
individual is for Thoreau a corollary of the destruction of nature.
Commitment, even to husbandry, offers dissipation rather than fulfillment;
and such indulgence, by weakening the body, enslaves and ultimately
extinguishes the spirit. Thoreau's report of his attempt at husbandry
parallels his account of hunting: both offered necessary learning
experiences on the way to an adulthood of restrained admiration for the
natural world. Richard Slotkin has observed that in Thoreau the
myth-type of the hunter was transformed into the naturalist rather than the
farmer.[5] That the naturalist has a bachelor's relation to nature, as Emer-

son saw, becomes clear when we set Thoreau's bean patch alongside Wendell Berry's Kentucky farm.

Whereas Thoreau could still lay claim to America's newness and find in it reason to reject the destructive materialism and commercialism that was beginning to dominate our culture, Berry belongs to a generation long past such innocence. In "A Native Hill," an early essay about his farm, Berry acknowledges that his "understanding of what is best for it is the tragic understanding of hindsight, the awareness that I have been taught what was here to be lost by the loss of it" (*Recollected Essays* 98). The first chapter of *Walden* has been described as "a diagnosis of [the] cultural malady Thoreau found in Concord".[6] A twentieth-century Thoreau must acknowledge this malady as heritage. Hence, *Clearing* opens with a poem entitled "History" in which the narrator, "long hunter and child" (4), carries the burden of the white man's history in America:

> I have arrived here
> many times. I have come
> on foot, on horseback, by boat
> and by machine—by earth,
> water, air, and fire.
> I came with axe and rifle.
> I came with a sharp eye
> and the price of land. I came
> in bondage, and I came
> in freedom unworth the name. (4-5)[7]

Berry is the hunter become farmer, husbandman. A kinsman to the bachelor of an earlier generation, he has taken up residence with his family where his older relative sojourned:

> Through my history's despite
> and ruin, I have come
> to its remainder, and here
> have made the beginning
> of a farm. (5)

Much of Berry's writing has been done in a rebuilt cabin, adjacent to Lanes Landing Farm, originally constructed by a bachelor uncle Berry admired in childhood. Berry tells the history of his association with this place in "The Long-Legged House," where he recalls his uncle "as a sort of wanderer visiting in the family households . . . a man . . . without either a home or a profession, and a teller of wonderful bedtime stories" (*Recollected Essays* 17). Berry was still a boy when his uncle died, and so he now surmises that "the best reason for the cabin he built here must be that it was in his nature to have a house in the woods and to return now and again to live in it. For there was in him something quiet-loving and solitary and kin to the river and the woods" (19). Berry discovered the place for himself in his youth and camped, hunted, and fished there. He and his wife spent the first months of their married life in this cabin; and later, they were able to purchase the farm lying next to it. Berry wonders what his uncle thought about alone in this cabin. "What desires and dreams came to him in his solitudes? Had he read Thoreau, I wonder—or any of the other writers and poets who have so shaped my life? I doubt it, and feel in that a large difference between us" (22).

Another large difference, of course, is that Berry has settled, whereas his uncle only camped out occasionally. Although Berry spent many solitary hours of his youth in this cabin, and again as a writer, he also brought his bride there to live. But the place offered a rich legacy, forming a bond between the youthful nephew, later a married man, and the solitary bachelor who bequeathed it. Thoreau, too, was "a sort of wanderer visiting in the family households" who left the legacy of a cabin in the woods. Berry's relationship to his bachelor uncle suggests the nature of his psychic kinship with Thoreau, from whom the legacy has also been rich while large differences remain.[8] Having been tutored in his view of nature and its ways by a bachelor kinsman who sojourned there, Berry has brought to nature his marriage, commitment, and the acts and understandings of husbandry.[9]

The greatest difference between Berry and Thoreau is the difference between bachelor and husband, between naturalist and farmer. Unlike Thoreau who would "live free and uncommitted," Berry insists on commitment, husbandry, the marriage of agriculture that links "nature and culture, the wild and the domestic." He has examined the theoretical implications of this marriage in *The Unsettling of America* and the practical implications in *The Gift of Good Land* and other essays. He has explored the experience in his novels, especially *A Place on Earth* and *The Memory of Old Jack*, and has celebrated marriage in his poetry, especially *Farming: A Hand Book*, *The Country of Marriage*, and *A Part*. *Clearing* offers history and personal experience, in labor and love, as vision, poetry. Berry's is not an easy commitment; in "Work Song," the pivotal poem in *Clearing*, he presents the dream of living free and uncommitted as well as the cost of commitment. "I have believed that I would never / have to forsake anything," he says; and he acknowledges dreaming that a "strange / woman ... / would beckon from her door, and even / in my hurry to reach her home her song / would draw me out of my way" (34). But he concludes,

> It is not to be. It is not to be.
> . . . .
> This steep, half-ruined, lovely place,
> this graced and wearing labor
> longer than my life, this marriage,
> blessed and difficult—these have
> a partial radiance that is all my light. (35)[10]

Clearing is not patterned after *Walden*, though it offers many instances for comparison. In *Walden's* first two chapters, "Economy" and "Where I Lived and What I Lived For," Thoreau identifies his place in the world and his reasons for being there—offering at once a cultural definition and a physical description that set him apart from and yet establish his relation to his neighbors. Berry's first two poems in *Clearing*, "History" and "Where," similarly set forth the author's place in culture and geography, though Berry's concern is more directly with ancestors than neighbors. Thoreau then follows a seasonal pattern to recount his experience and "suck out all the marrow of life" (91), emerging at last with "Spring" and "Conclusion," which confirm our sense of how much the dawn, the day, the sun, and spring have warmed even his most wintry chapters. *Clearing* moves through all seasons in its seven long poems but is dominated by winter. It is winter when the first poem begins, with the narrator leaving for a place he does not know:

> The crops were made. The leaves
> were down. Three frosts had lain
> upon the broad stone
> step beneath the door. (3)

And it is winter's end that ends the book. Spring calls the poet from his words to his fields, but winter's sense of an ending offers the concluding theme. Surrounded by songs of spring and green fields, the poet must leave "this warm light room, where words / have kept me through the cold days"; he "must turn away / from books" (52).[11] The first two poems of *Clearing* are followed by "The Clearing" and "Work Song," poems answering a supplication in "History": "Let what is in the flesh / O Muse, be brought to mind" (6). But whereas Thoreau awakes in spring after bringing flesh to mind in his fashion, Berry follows "Work Song" with two dream-like, night-dominated poems, "The Bed" and "The Crest." And he ends with "Reverdure," a poem that contains no promise of an external dawn and sunrise, but rather brings to the fore the necessary harmony of life and death in the cycles of nature's reproduction and man's participation in them.

These oppositions of night and winter in *Clearing* with day and spring in *Walden* adumbrate meaningful distinctions between the two works, their authors' views of man's relation to nature, and the generations of American history that produced the two works. But neither Berry nor Thoreau writes so simply (though with comparable clarity of style) that these are merely oppositions. The poetic density of Thoreau's sparkling prose conveys much more than optimistic sheen. Berry's poetry of night, death, and history's ruin carries to its deceptively prosaic surface a similarly ambiguous glimmer that bends us to the source of its light, to hope and life and health:

> All the lives this place
> has had, I have. I eat
> my history day by day.
>
> . . . .

> Now let me feed my song
> upon the life that is here
> that is the life that is gone. (5-6)

Berry approves of Thoreau's contention that poetry "is nothing but healthy speech" and notes that Thoreau "only in prose . . . could break free
into the presence of the life around him and become a poet" (*A Continuous
Harmony* 14, 28). The poems in *Clearing* reflect Berry's approval of
Thoreau's poetics. Long segments of "Where" record the previous owners
of Berry's farm in plain, spare language:

> Asa Batts kept it
> for only six years
> and in 1871 sold it
> —Sullinger's Landing had now
> become Lanes Landing—
> to A. J. & Matilda Jones,
> who divided it into two tracts
> of about ten and about
> forty acres each. (8)

But the lined structure and the accumulation of names, dates, and tract
sizes draw our attention by their "clarity and directness" and "painstaking
accuracy"—Berry's terms to describe the poetic qualities of Thoreau's
prose (*A Continuous Harmony* 29)—toward the latest entry in the record to
make it record much more than a legal transaction:

> On February 7, 1965
> it became our deed
> to which we put our names:
> Wendell and Tanya Berry. (10)[12]

By this precise date and the real names, the poet sheds his historical and
fictive persona; and the word *deed* is restored from dead legality to the sense
of a living act committed. Much as the "former inhabitants" of the land
near Walden Pond betray to Thoreau's readers the paltry transcience of

human activity in the face of nature's enduring continuity, so here the impermanence of legal transactions and human habitation are reflected against a land which endures but "bears the scars / of minds whose history / was submerged in numbers" (13-14).[13] Nevertheless, Berry says,

> There is a way to live
> in face of ignorance and greed.
> The way is the way of water,
> that patiently stays and fills
> the place it comes to, until
> a way is found. (19)[14]

Thus the Berrys, having purchased a portion of Lanes Landing, waited for an opportunity to wrest the remainder from destruction by a developer, and they were able to purchase the land by paying a high price in more ways then one:

> It is the price of vision
> that we owe, the cost
> of what has been here, what
> can be. By this we are lost
> to other possibility. In fear
> and hope, by work and sleep
> we are married here. (20)

The work of restoring this neglected, mistreated land is told in "The Clearing," where Berry offers a striking contrast to the "rare amusement" of Thoreau in his bean field. The poem opens with a listing of the varieties of the land's overgrowth, "all trees / that follow man's neglect" (21); and its first section ends with the startling invocation, "sing, chainsaw, the hard song / of vision cutting in" (21).[15] Section 2 explains: "Vision must have severity / at its edge: / against neglect, / . . . indifference, / . . . weariness" (21-22). Berry's vision is one of labor and commitment, of involvement in "the predicament of other lives" (23). In "his marriage married / to his place" (24), he knows that "labor is no preparation / but takes life as it goes / and casts upon it / death's shadow" (25). The farmer's labor is to "feed /

the lives that feed / lives" (26). This predicament affords recognition of his own mortality and its meaning: "Life / must be served" (26). But the act that puts meat on the table and defines mortality also carries a moral imperative. Just as the sounds of military demonstrations interrupted Thoreau in his bean field, other thoughts intrude on Berry's labor with life and death on the farm:

> Streets, guns, machines,
> quicker fortunes, quicker deaths
> bear down on these
> hills. . . .
> > The arrival
> may be complete in my time,
> and I will see the end
> of names: Tingle and Berry
> and Lanes. (27)[16]

He asks, "Then why clear / yet again an old farm?" (27). In his answer, Berry insists it is necessary to "make clear what was overgrown" and to "put it / back in mind" (28). To clear the land is to clear the mind; the agricultural act is a cultural—ecological—imperative.

Early in *Clearing* the poet has told us his farm is "intended to become / my art of being here," and he acknowledges that "until my song comes here / to learn its words, my art / is but the hope of song" (5). "Work Song," the fourth of the seven poems, is therefore centrally important as well as the middle poem in the book. It grows from the clearing of land and mind, and its six titled sections mirror in order the larger poems on either side of it. The first of these is "*A Lineage*," which begins, "By the fall of years I learn how it has been / With Jack Beechum, Mat Feltner, Elton Penn" (31). In apposition to the literal record, the historical names, and the prose-like verse of "History," Berry here calls to mind in rhymed couplets the chief fictional characters of his novels, "men made for their fields" as truly as Tingle, Berry, and Lanes. As "Where" recalls the purchase of the farm, "*A Vision*," the second section of "Work Song," imagines a future when "the lives our lives prepare will live / here" and "families will be singing in the fields" (32). "This is no paradisal dream," Berry says. "Its hardship is its possibility" (32). His work-hardened vision leads deeper in "*Passion*," the third section of "Work Song,"[17] where a fearful clearing of mind, of the overgrowth of imagination, counterbalances "The Clearing." An ancient passion—"beneath speech" (32)—leads him "beyond the words of books" (33) to a field where he stands "like a horse dumbly / approving of the grass" (33), and he is "curious and afraid / one day my poems may pass / through my mind unwritten" (33). This, too, is a clearing; it is also as severe a vision as that which led him into the woods with a chainsaw. What is fearful about this passion that brings silence, this polar attraction of nature in the wild, is that it draws him too far to one end of agriculture's field of force between the wild and the domestic, nature and culture. But nature also offers a way back to culture:

> Some days I wait here
> empty as a tree
> whose birds and leaves
> have gone. And I know my words
> have gone in search of things. (34)

With this passion now understood as a hunt from which the hunter must return home, Berry can go on to "*Forsaking All Others*," a section I quoted earlier, an intensely moving, dark lyric in which he overcomes temptation to accept "a partial radiance that is all [his] light" (35). In the next section, "*A Beginning*," he moves beyond the measure of personal darkness he has accepted to a consideration of the cultural darkness around us (and these sections together anticipate the two night-dominated poems following "Work Song"):

> October's completing light falls
> on the unfinished patterns of my year.
> The sun is yellow in a smudge
> of public lies we no longer try
> to believe. Speech finally drives us
> to silence. . . .
>   We are
> a people who must decline or perish. (35)

But Berry's prophecy is no more a reason to despair than Thoreau's equally hard vision of a culture of frugality informed by nature is a paradisal dream. For Berry, "human vision begins its rise / in the dark of seeds, wombs of beasts" (35); and having reached "the silence at the tongue's root / in which speech begins," he concludes the section with a new resolve:

> Let my words then begin in labor.
> Let me sing a work song
> and an earth song. Let the song of light
> fall upon me as it may. (36)

"*Returning to the Beloved*," the final section of "Work Song," is the most lyrical piece in the book. It is, finally, a song—about work done, not a vision imagined—a love/work song in four-line, rhymed stanzas. And the work is that of hauling manure onto the frost-hardened autumn fields with a team of horses (an act of "reverdure," as Berry will explain in the book's final poem):

> And now we make this return, the team
> And I. In the glimmering atmosphere of song
> We come and go again, rebuilding promise
> In the ground. It will not be long
>
> Before the cold will drive us in. But this, now
> Is where I ought to be, and want to be,
> And where I am. Desire and circumstance
> Are one. Like a woman's arms this work holds me. (36)

Like a dream or riddle, the next poem, "The Bed,"[18] conjures forth a scene of ancient hunters (or perhaps warriors) camped in the fields, one of them dying. It is winter when "the ground's a grave, and so / it thrives," hiding "the seeds, in whose dark / the future and the past / internested lie" (37). After the wounded man's death and burial by his companions, "the place again / is as it was, night filling it" (39). In death he will nourish the earth, "the valley wider by his body's width" (39). The last segment of "The Bed" raises the dead to mind, to song, in short, rhymed couplets:

Like the fields, my mind's a bed.
Graves open in my head.

The dead rise and walk about
The timeless fields of thought.
. . . .
To sorrow, their death is long.
Their coming again is song. (39-40)

"My subjects are my objects," Berry announced at the beginning, and throughout *Clearing* he turns over and over the couplings that shape and govern the movement of his poems: beginning, end; past, future; flesh, mind; work, rest; day, night; song, silence; husband, wife; life, death. "From the Crest," the penultimate poem, suggests the moment occupied by the stasis of a wave's peak. It is a poem that places sleep in the context of work, and death in the context of life. "What we leave behind to sleep," Berry says, "is ahead of us when we wake" (41). This moment of rest restores the past and prepares the future. Hence, "My life's wave is at its crest. / The thought of work becomes / a friend of the thought of rest" (42). The bed of rest is also the lovebed; and the climax of love, like rest, or the crest of life, is both release and the beginning of something. "The farm must be made a form," Berry says, in an association of words as common to dreaming as poetry, by the "delight that moves / lovers in their loves" (43). In this moment he is "trying to teach my mind / to bear the long, slow growth / of the fields" (42) and—because "the grave is in sight" (43) from the crest, and any bed may be a deathbed—

to accept the finish
that all good work must have:
of hands touching me,
days and weathers passing
over me, the smooth of love,
the wearing of the earth. (43)

In the dreamlike state of this poem, Berry speaks to his "little farm," thus speaking:

> to myself, for we are one
> body. When I speak to you,
> I speak to wife, daughter, son,
> . . . .
> to all that brotherhood that rises
> daily in your substance
> and walks, burrows, flies, stands. (44)

But this union of subject with object, farmer with farm, like the act of love or the resolution of sleep, like our lives on earth, is momentary, "held in place / by vision, love, and work, / all as passing as a thought" (45). And in the winter night "the farm travels in snow" while "the dead and living / prepare again to mate" (47).

"Reverdure is my calling," Berry proclaims in the final poem,[19] "to make these scars grow" (50). The uncommon word, *reverdure*, titles the poem and gives a name to the marriage bond formed by farmer and farm, nature and culture, flesh and mind. Reverdure is reproductive: what the soil grows it eats again; lives feed lives; matter begets mind, and mind nourishes matter. "The way in prepares / the way out" (48), Berry says; and the end of the book recalls its beginning:

> And so, in the first warmth of the year,
> I went up with saw and axe
> to cut a way in. I made a road, I made
> a thought-way under the trees. (51)

But history's ruin and the continually renewing act of reclearing the land and the mind have taught him to leave a steep woods "standing, a part / of the farm not farmed, / its sacred grove" (52). The troubling presence of mystery, the darkness of mind, is resolved by nature's example: "there are ways / the deer walk in darkness / that are clear" (52). And so the time comes to make "an end to words / for a while—for this time, / or for all time. Any end may last" (52). The coming of winter brought a work song while the poet / farmer completed the acts of the farming year, hauling manure onto the fields in October. The coming of spring brings the need to tend the farm and end the poem.

This poet's farm is no hobby, or garden of metaphors; this farmer's thought is not idle musing. In agriculture — Berry's vision of agriculture — nature and culture are married. Thus has the husbandman kept and extended his bachelor uncle's clearing. *Clearing* is "healthy speech," as hopeful as Thoreau's dawning sun; it deserves space beside *Walden* in the register of our cultural deeds.

NOTES

1 *Wendell Berry's Husband to the World:* A Place on Earth, *American Literature* 51 (1979):239. [Nibbelink lists Berry's work between 1980 and 1983: *Ed.*]

2 *A Week on the Concord and Merrimack Rivers*, ed. Carl F. Hovde, in *Writings of Henry D. Thoreau* (Princeton,N.J., 1980), p.54.

3 *Clearing* (New York, 1977), p.2. [Reprinted in *Collected Poems 1957-1982*, in a revised text. The prologue is not included: *Ed.*]

4 *Walden* ed. J. Lyndon Shanley, in *The Writings of Henry D. Thoreau* (Princeton, N.J., 1971), pp.3, 90.

5 *Regeneration through Violence* (Middleton, Conn., 1973), pp.519-21.

6 Leo Marx, *The Machine in the Garden* (New York, 1967), p.247.

7 [In *Collected Poems*. "unworth" is amended to "not worth": *Ed.*]

8 Speer Morgan, "Wendell Berry: A Fatal Singing," *Southern Review* 10 (1974): 865-877, emphasizes the differences between Thoreau and an earlier Berry and casts Thoreau as a Romantic monk. I prefer Emerson's view of him as a Protestant bachelor.

9 While preparing this essay, I shared some of my early thoughts about it with Mr. Berry. His response included the following: "It's the connection between nature and culture, the wild and the domestic, that concerns me (agriculture *is* such a connection...) and I don't think Thoreau can help much with that. But he went far beyond the Romantic poets as an observer and understander and advocate of nature, and he is indispensible to us for that" (letter, 1 Jan. 1982).

10 [These lines are not included in *Collected Poems*: *Ed.*]

11 [Not in *Collected Poems*: *Ed.*]

12 [This and the previous quotation not in *Collected Poems*: *Ed.*]

13 [In *Collected Poems* this passage is revised to read: "bears the scars / of minds whose history / was imprinted by no example / of a forebearing mind, corrected, / beloved.": *Ed.*]

14 [This and the following quotation not in *Collected Poems*: *Ed.*]

15 [The revised text in *Collected Poems* reads "sing, steel, the hard song...": *Ed.*]

16 [The names are omitted in *Collected Poems*: *Ed.*]

17 ["*Passion*", "*Forsaking All Others*", and "*Returning to the Beloved*" not in *Collected Poems*: *Ed.*]

18 [Not in *Collected Poems*: *Ed.*]

19 [Not in *Collected Poems*: *Ed.*]

The Where, How, Who and the What in Wendell Berry's Writing

Ross Feld

In "Thicker Than Liquor," a plumb-lined story from Berry's collection *The Wild Birds*, a young man repeatedly is called away from his Port William, Kentucky home to Louisville, to bail out, to extricate, a drunken uncle. In time the repetition of the act takes over from the obligation, the circuit of the doing and the done-for becoming a belt smoothly, equally weighted everywhere. Nephew and sodden uncle stop owing one another for anything as their comedy turns, foremostly, into a convincing (to them and us) human rhythm.

This rhythm isn't uncommon in Berry's work. The regularity of its beat is a tonic against the anxiety of constant originality (which it denies—everything we do is done again, and has been done before) and, more pointedly, lays a certain ghost to rest. The ghost is thankfulness.

Thankfulness is the most unassuagable of our thirsts. We grow up in hopeful expectation that what we do will be appreciated—at the very least acknowledged. Modern egos don't naturally hurl themselves into the nothingness of the future without half counting on some reward of notice. Acknowledgement, or the lack of it, even is the very subtext of our fascination with nature—its infinity and serene ignorance of our rapture. Maybe because he's a farmer and thus unburdened of the romance of the natural sublime, or maybe simply because he is a man unusually interested in the dynamics of piety and impiety, Berry has tried with some success to fashion a side of his work as an argument against these expectations and inevitable disappointments. He seems instead to want to try to make peace with a world that eternally will be just barely enough: that will stingily provide and allow ground—and ground only—on which we can then make our better and worse efforts.

As someone urbanly, Jewishly unlanded, I'm tuned-in only to a little of what Berry's respect for the local and the landed means to him. But the part of it I do understand seems to me an homage to horizontality. The verticals rightly belong to God, which we humans suffer in the forms of fear and humility, things that are in Berry's work aplenty: as ultimates will, they pin him down and lay him low. But work (be it farming, marriage, writing, friendship, neighborliness, meaning, attending) is the horizon of a non-ultimate, daily human life. It stretches outward far beyond any one arm's reach, where it is spent and distributed, and *does not reconstitute in a humanly satisfying way, ever.*

For a long time I've suspected that if Berry wrote in an eastern-European language—and we knew that we were reading him in translation—his Nobel already would be on the stove, cooking. The particular quality of dis-illusion in Berry, unbaited with expectation, is profoundly free. Why this fascinating and paradoxical tone—of consciously repetitious freedom—gets so often missed by otherwise discerning readers I don't know. Of course Berry's life is unusual, that of a non-urban farming writer who writes about things like topsoil. So we fasten him down as an agrarian, someone under the spell of the Where.

But this is to read him not finely enough (also, incidentally, to overvalue the Where). Even Wordsworth understood that the Where itself can't fully nourish a Who. Berry is interested rather in a *Who in-relation,* a Who never truly singular but communal, either overtly or subtly—through repetition. That repetition, his work says, will be unavoidable as long as there is an existential referent, natural or Godly, that refuses to acknowledge.

It's a Who that becomes a sort of What. As deeply in love with our "inner lives" as most of are, with our own personal thank-you machines, we could do without this simultaneously elasticized and parceled-out and objectified Who that Berry writes with. We want to push it to the sidelines and tag Berry a Tolstoyan throwback, a crank, a Christian. Yet the large hard unfashionable thing he has worked at coheres: the fitting of a Who that's more like a What back into contemporary life and thereby providing a figure of true, free, yet helplessly repeatable humanity American writers don't often find a way to propose as artfully.

Remembering
and Home Defense

Carl D. Esbjornson

Wendell Berry considers literature a form of "home defense." He maintains that "its real habitat is the household and the community" and "that it can and does affect, even in practical ways, the life of a place" (*What Are People For?* 84). Berry sets up his literary practice as a form of cultural stewardship, revealing the wisdom behind an acute understanding of "the human necessities and the human limits" (*The Unsettling of America* 43) and clarifying the life-enhancing values of good literature, good work, "kindly use" of the land, neighborliness (sharing stories, tools, work, advice, joy, grief), and staying in place.

Staying in place is most crucial; if people move away, then what Wes Jackson calls "cultural information" is lost (*Altars of Unhewn Stone* 11). That is why after several years of being away, studying and teaching, writing and travelling, Berry returned to Kentucky in 1964 and bought a hillside farm near where he grew up and where his grandfather farmed: "It occurred to me that there was another measure for my life than the amount and quality of the writing I did; a man, I thought, must be judged by how willingly and meaningfully he can be present where he is, by how fully he can make himself at home in his part of the world" (*The Hidden Wound* 87). Berry makes yet another crucial point about the nature and importance of this work: people who have local allegiances, living and working to sustain thriving communities, "defend the country daily and hourly in all their acts by taking care of it, by causing it to thrive, by giving it the health and satisfactions that make it worth defending, and by teaching these things to the young" (*Home Economics* 109). Good farming, as Berry sees it, exemplifies one form of home defense, for it is ecologically and culturally sustainable—that is, people stay on the land to make sure that it is well cared for and that their knowledge of care and affection is passed on to others.

For Berry, literary practice is a part of this work, intimately tied to a sense of place and valuable for what it teaches; it is also a repository of accumulated wisdom, part of what his mentor, Wallace Stegner, calls "the great community of recorded human experience" (quoted in *What Are People For?* 50) and a way of retaining "cultural information." This is strikingly true of Berry's latest novel, *Remembering;* the work draws upon a rich literary and cultural heritage, one that includes Dante, Milton, Homer and, most important of all, the local wisdom of Berry's "part of the world," Port Royal, Kentucky, and its fictional incarnation, Port William.

Dante figures most prominently, for *Remembering* is a retelling of Dante's epic of spiritual dismemberment and healing, with its small doses of humor and satire, its comic mode, and its profound analysis of the process of psychic healing and recapitulation following spiritual crisis. It is a poet's novel, opening *in medias res* with an obvious Miltonic allusion and a subtle, unmistakable reference to the opening lines of Dante's *Commedia:*

> It is dark. He does not know where he is. And then he sees pale light from the street soaking in above the drawn drapes. It is not a light to see by, but only makes the darkness visible. He has slept, to his surprise, but has wakened in the same unease that kept him sleepless long after he went to bed and that remained with him in dream (*Remembering* 4).

Thus Andy Catlett, the main character, awakes in *una selva oscura*, in a San Francisco hotel room, a long way from his home in Port William. Andy is literally astray: after an ignominious outburst at a university-sponsored agriculture conference in the midwest, where he denounced the proceedings rather than delivering his paper, he has come to San Francisco for a speaking engagement at a local college, but failed to keep his appointment. He lies in bed, measuring his psychic distance from home, recalling the quarrel, one full of self-pity, that he had with his wife, Flora, before he left.

Andy realizes the extent of his alienation because of the dream he just had of the destruction of Port William, the bulldozing of its fields and the driving off of its inhabitants. The man responsible for this destruction, a self-proclaimed "hard-headed realist," is sitting at a desk devouring himself, saying, "'Neighbors? I have no neighbors. Friends? I have no friends. This is my independence. This is my victory'" (4). This dream image of American radical individualism and self-interested economic determinism, which, Berry contends, is responsible for destroying American agriculture and, with it, rural homes and communities, awakens Andy to another more essential truth—of sin as separation. This separation is so profound that, like Ugolino devouring his sons in *Inferno XXXIII*, a person assents to the destruction of even those things that were once most beloved.

In Berry's novel, re-membering is the necessary means of spiritual healing; Andy's psychic dismemberment is the result of physical dismemberment—his right hand had been amputated after a corn picker accident—a separation as permanent as Dante's exile proved to be. This accident is another reflection of the self-devouring man in Andy's dream; Andy's hand is devoured by a machine, underscoring Berry's point that machines should not be allowed "to replace people, or to replace or reduce human skills" (*The Unsettling of America* 90). More crucially, Andy's dismemberment engenders a bitterness and rage that severs him from his family, especially from Flora (a word-play, in addition to the name's obvious associations, on Dante's home city, Florence?), from the deep satisfactions of his life's work of farming, and from his sense of rootedness with Port William, and, perhaps most crucially, from himself:

> His right hand had been the one with which he reached out to
> the world and attached himself to it. When he lost his hand he
> lost his hold. It was as though his hand still clutched all that
> was dear to him—and was gone. All the world then became to

> him a steep slope, and he a man descending, staggering and
> falling, unable to reach out to tree trunk or branch or root to
> catch and hold on. (*Remembering* 28)

Andy's good left hand serves only to exacerbate his alienation, making
familiar tasks unfamiliar. This disorientation, imaged by "all the world
became a steep slope," recalls Dante's backsliding in the opening canto of
Inferno where the three beasts force him down the steep slope as he repeatedly tries to climb it.

Dante's spiritual confusion takes him through Hell, where he confronts
and comes to terms with the dislocations of Italy's—and Florence's—strife-
ridden history and achieves the self-understanding necessary to his even-
tual spiritual redemption. Andy's way takes him through agricultural history, *and* through personal and family history as it relates to the local history
of Port William. He, too, begins his journey of spiritual regeneration in a
modern hell—the agriculture conference. In Berry's satirical rendering of
this conference, Andy's shorthand notes turn the utterances of the conferees into a kind of infernal gibberish: "'4. Grvlng in rth. Big biz. Amnty of lf:
TV. Trdoffs: fam, cmmnty, nghbrs, soil, wtr. Prc of prg. Adpt or die. Gt bg
or gt out. Fr mkt. 1 to 70. Fd wrld. Weapon'" (*Remembering* 12). These notes
distill the standard clichés and justifications for mainstream industrial agriculture in a paper delivered by a high official in the U.S. Department of
Agriculture whose career, despite the disclaimer at the beginning of the
novel, strongly resembles that of former U.S. Secretary of Agriculture Earl
Butz, the *bête noire* of Berry's brilliant critique of American (agri)culture, *The
Unsettling of America*. For Berry, contemporary American agricultural history
is, in Henry Adams' terms, "immoral and incoherent," in other words, a
kind of moral gibberish. Since World War II, this history consists of the displacement of millions of rural Americans in the name of social, technologi-
cal, and economic "progress" and the consequent rise of a professional elite
in government, academia, and the agribusiness industry.

In Andy's (and Berry's) Hell, these professionals are exemplars, in Hannah Arendt's phrase, of "the banality of evil," for these are ordinary people,
simply doing their jobs, establishing their careers without regard to the
consequences of their work. In order to pass his spiritual nadir and enact
his psychic redemption, Andy, when it is his turn to speak, abandons his

prepared text and takes his stand, excoriating the conferees for their hygienically academic habits of thought that, in the interest of profit and career advancement, lay to waste "actual fields and farms and actual human lives" (*Remembering* 24). While delivering his denunciation, Andy tells a story about an injustice committed against his grandparents, who had taken their yearly harvest to the warehouse and, instead of earning a profit, ended up owing $3.57. "'I think that bill came out of a room like this,' Andy said, 'where a family's life and work can be converted to numbers and to somebody else's profit, but the family cannot be seen and its suffering cannot be felt'" (*Remembering* 25).

Andy's denunciation demonstrates a point that we should not overlook: Wendell Berry, like Andy, comes from a family of lawyers as well as farmers. And Berry has the mind of a lawyer whose moral passion is cut to a fine edge by a gift for keen, incisive argumentation. Perhaps this explains, as well, his literary practice as a kind of "home defense." The fidelity of word and truth so central to his essay, "Standing by Words," is central to his way of standing up to the destruction of American rural life, which, to Berry, amounts to a betrayal of American political ideals. In his essay, "Think Little," he says, "I am ashamed and deeply distressed that American government should have become the chief cause of disillusionment with American principles" (*A Continuous Harmony* 75). Berry stands by those principles in forming his critique of the "sorry practice" of the policy makers in the government; one of his methods is to expose their duplicity:

> I remember, during the fifties, the outrage with which our political leaders spoke of the forced removal of the populations of villages in communist countries. I also remember that at the same time, in Washington, the word on farming was "Get big or get out"—a policy which is still in effect and which has taken an enormous toll. The only difference is that of method: the force used by the communists was military; with us, it has been economic—a "free market" in which the freest were the richest. The attitudes are equally cruel, and I believe that the results will prove equally damaging, not just to the concerns and values of the human spirit, but to the practicalities of survival. (*The Unsettling of America* 41)

Berry's point is that American political leaders go against their word by no longer offering a true alternative to totalitarianism according to the high moral standards set by the Jeffersonian ideal of an independent citizenry. Instead they reward those few who contribute to and profit from the centralization of economic and political power. In this way, Berry functions, much like Dante, as an upholder of moral standards, and as an arbiter, like the country lawyer, who takes a stand for rural folk against those interests that want to exploit them. We see this in "Think Little," when he vows that the next time he leads a delegation to present a petition against the strip mining of coal to the governor he will be there "not with a sign or a slogan or a button, but with the facts and the arguments" (*A Continuous Harmony* 75). As a writer, Berry truly intends to establish the "necessary and indispensible connection between language and truth, and therefore between language and deeds" according to the "precedent" (we should note Berry's choice of words) of "the Christian idea of the Incarnate Word, the Word entering the world as flesh, and inevitably therefore as action" (*Standing by Words* 30). Thus what Berry says of Harry Caudill, a true country lawyer who has spoken out against strip mining in eastern Kentucky, also applies to Berry himself: "[Harry Caudill] did not come there [to Letcher County, Kentucky], then, to serve justice. He has been there because he has belonged there; the land and people for whom he has spoken are his own" (*What Are People For?* 33).

However, for Andy, mere denunciation, even in defense of his people, does not ensure his psychic redemption; that comes in remembering the stories of actual people in an actual place that are part of his own life story, and in bringing his past into the continuity of his present. This remembering resumes while he walks the streets of San Francisco after leaving his hotel room. As the darkness gives way to the light of dawn, he remembers the exemplary values of neighborliness, hard work, generational wisdom (especially on how to farm and care for the land), and a strong sense of community on the part of his ancestors, his family, and the other inhabitants of Port William. In a moment of epiphany, Andy sees the following inscription on a church: "LA GLORIA DI COLUI CHE TUTTO MUOVE PER L'UNIVERSO PENETRA E RISPLENDE" (*Remembering* 48). This inscription, the opening lines of Dante's *Paradiso*, is echoed in the final words of the chapter: "But the whole bay is shining now, the islands, the city on its hills, the wooden houses and towers, the green treetops, the flashing waves and wings, the glory that moves all things resplendent everywhere" (*Remembering* 59).

With this, Andy emerges from his darkness and the next chapter begins with a moment of Dantean resolution: "Though he has not moved, he has turned. I must go now" (*Remembering* 60). This recalls Dante's reversal in *Inferno XXXIV*, when, while climbing down Satan's leg, he passed the center of gravity and suddenly found himself ascending, toward Purgatory. From here, the novel begins its long denouement; by re-membering, Andy gives himself back to Port William. In time, Andy makes his peace with the hook that has replaced his right hand—"It is a tool" (*Remembering* 70). This peace is echoed in the ecstatic close of the novel: "Their [the inhabitants of Port William] names singing in his mind, he lifts toward them the restored right hand of his joy" (*Remembering* 124). Even without his hand, he is able to get hold of a world that is once again familiar and familial, to gain re-membership with all the living and dead members of the "blessed circle" in the communal order of Port William. Moreover, the hook, because Andy thinks of it as a tool, is no longer a symbol of Andy's alienation; for "tool" is a loaded term in Berry's lexicon, designating something that, according to Berry's standard of appropriate—or "kindly"—use, enhances, rather than destroys, the connection between life and work.

In order to arrive at a just critical understanding of *Remembering*, we should note that the novel draws on epic tradition rather than the conventions of the modern novel. Berry's discontinuous narrative structure not only reflects episodic epic form, but corresponds with the asynchronic act of re-membering; furthermore, this technique serves a didactic function by juxtaposing exemplars of good and bad conduct, in a way that recalls the methodology of Pound's *Cantos*, and Dante, as well as the earlier epic tradition. Accordingly, Mat Feltner and Andy's father, Wheeler, are exemplars of the good, for they return to serve Port William rather than leaving it permanently after receiving their college educations. In rendering the scene where Mat Feltner decides to stay home after finishing college, Berry presents us with the suggestive image of Mat's wife coming toward him, "her long skirt gathered in one hand to keep it out of the dew" (*Remembering*

63). This recalls the dew that Dante uses in his ritualistic washing away of sin in *Purgatorio I;* Mat, in making this decision, washed himself of what for Berry is one of the great sins committed in American life—the idea that one must leave home in order to have a satisfying career. Accordingly, the participants in the agriculture conference are exemplars of the bad, for they use education to serve their self-interested goal of career advancement, not caring that they use their educations to destroy the farms and communities they left behind. This method of turning characters into exemplars is the main feature of the fifth chapter, "A Place Known and Dreamed," a crucial remembering in Andy's journey of psychic redemption. Andy recalls the "conversion experience" that brought him back to Port William after he left there as a young man to pursue a journalism career in San Francisco. He ended up working as an agricultural journalist for *Scientific Farming,* work he enjoyed up to the day he visited a model (by the standards of *Scientific Farming*) two thousand-acre modern industrial farm he had been assigned to write about. This farm was planted in a typical corn monoculture where "there was not a fence, not an animal, not a woodlot, not a tree, not a garden" (*Remembering* 73). Bill Meikelberger, the farm's owner, reveals, with the candor of one of Dante's damned souls, a spiritual impoverishment summed up in his permanent debt, the only way to fund a huge modern farming operation, and his ulcer, the product of considerable financial worry. Berry cannot resist editorial comment: "Meikelberger's ambition had made common cause with a technical power that imposed no limit to itself, that was, in fact, destroying Meikelberger, as it had already destroyed nearly all that was natural or human around him" (*Remembering* 76). In Berry's typology, Meikelberger is the self-devouring man in Andy's dream. After this visit, Andy wonders whether he can write an article praising modern farming in good conscience; he takes the back roads toward home and happens into Amish country where he stops to talk with an Amish farmer, Isaac Troyer, who subsequently invites him to dinner. In juxtaposition with the sterile monoculture of the Meikelberger farm, Berry presents the teeming diversity of the much smaller Amish farm:

> He saw that the buildings were painted and in good repair.
> He saw the garden, newly worked and partly planted behind

the house. He saw the martin boxes by the garden, and the small orchard with beehives under the trees. He saw fifteen guernsey cows and two more black mares in a pasture. He saw a stallion in a paddock beside the barn, and behind the barn a pen from which he could hear the sounds of pigs. He saw hens scratching in a large poultry yard. (*Remembering* 80)

This scene is contrived to underscore how the farming methods of the Amish are demonstrably superior, culturally and ecologically, to those of modern "scientific" farmers. In the Meikelberger home, Andy notes the partiality of life there, the modern and unused kitchen, and Meikelberger's wife whom Andy never meets because she has an off-farm job. In contrast, Andy does meet Isaac's wife, and sees that the kitchen is well used in serving up a satisfying dinner. Berry's editorial voice breaks in once again to make a telling point:

Twenty-five [Amish] families like Isaac Troyer's could have farmed and thrived—could have made a healthy, comely, independent community—on the two thousand acres where Bill Meikelberger lived virtually alone with his ulcer, the best friend that the bank and the farm machinery business and the fertilizer business and the oil companies and the chemical companies ever had. (*Remembering* 84)

Andy parts company with *Scientific Farming* over the article on Bill Meikelberger. His quarrel with its editor, Tommy Netherbough, reaches its climax in the form of neatly balanced thesis and antithesis, with Tommy speaking first and Andy countering:

"Meikelberger's the future of American agriculture."
"Meikelberger's the end of American agriculture—the end of the future." (*Remembering* 85)

Andy is on the "losing" side of this argument. Even so, he is resolute: "But that an argument was losing did not mean that it should not be made" (*Remembering* 87).

And isn't "standing by words" at the heart of Andy's choice? The key to Andy's "conversion experience" is not simply that he awakens to the wrongs of modern industrial agriculture, but that he acts upon his realization by leaving *Scientific Farming* and coming home again: "He was not arguing for himself, and not just for Isaac and Anna Troyer [the Amish couple he visited]. He was arguing his father's argument" (*Remembering* 86). Andy acts according to an important precedent: his father's argument, and the values that inform it, emanate from character-building struggles, most importantly the father's decision to come home after passing up a splendid opportunity to advance his career as a lawyer in Chicago.

This fidelity to place and to the life of a community is necessary to another of Berry's great concerns, the establishment of a household in the good faith mutuality of marriage. When Andy tells Flora that he has left *Scientific Farming* and wants to return home, she replies, "Well, it's about time" (*Remembering* 92). Flora's reply represents a coming home of a different sort. Berry raises a point in his superb statement, "Poetry and Marriage," that particularily applies to her: "One does not care for this ground to make it a different place, or to make it perfect, but to make it inhabitable and to make it better. To flee from its realities is only to arrive at them unprepared" (*Standing by Words* 200). The establishment of a household in the communality of marriage is also crucial to the resolution of Andy's crisis. Like Penelope in *The Odyssey*, Flora prepares for the return of her wayward husband from San Francisco by tending steadfastly to the household. When Andy returns, he finds the farm and household in good order and well cared for.

Thus Berry draws instructively on literary tradition to underscore his point about restoring the necessary bonds between human beings and places. Even though the other characters are flat as a result of making Andy the center of consciousness in the novel—they serve more as types in keeping with epic tradition—the result is an insightful account of Andy's crisis, which, like Dante's, comes in the midst of life. The novel's most salient point is that Andy overcomes his alienation because he still has a place, a household, and a community with its own rich history, to draw him back. For Berry, people's lives are most viable and best nurtured in the context of "a history, a community, and a place" (*Home Economics* 118).

These qualities are captured with affecting simplicity in Flora's note that Andy finds upon his return:

> You're back?
> Mart called. They have lots of beans.
> We've gone to pick and visit.
> Love,
> F.   (*Remembering* 119)

Embodied here is a stability that makes return possible: Flora, because she can share work and conversation with neighbors, has a life that is meaningful on its own terms, even in Andy's absence. We see that she does not even have to suffer through Andy's crisis of self, because Flora has a life within, not without, the context of a community that enables her to go on about *familiar* business. A marriage, Berry is telling us, can best thrive—or survive—within this context. For this reason, Flora is able to ride out Andy's crisis and prepare for his return.

Berry especially wants his readers to understand this point. When leaving home is the norm, the shared work and life of the common culture, a source of strength in Flora and Andy's marriage, is taken over by the misnamed "popular culture" (*What Are People For?* 118), which consists of the entertainment industry and national consumerism, empowered by the art of advertising and supported by the education industry. The cost of this is the uprooting of local cultures and local economies, resulting in broken marriages and the social ills in back of the profound sense of alienation characteristic of modern American life. In "The Work of Local Culture," Berry fleshes out the assumptions behind this deracination:

> And by now the transformation of the ancient story is nearly complete. Our society, on the whole, has forgotten or repudiated the theme of return. Young people still grow up in rural families and go off to the cities, not to return. But now it is felt that this is what they *should* do. Now the norm is to leave and not return. . . .
> . . . And this norm is institutionalized not in great communal

stories, but in the education system. The schools are no longer
oriented to a cultural inheritance that is their duty to pass on
unimpaired, but to the career, which is to say the future, of the
child. The orientation is thus necessarily theoretical, specula-
tive, and mercenary. The child is not educated to return home
and be of use to the place and community; he or she is educated to *leave* home and earn money in a provisional future that
has nothing to do with place or community. And parents with
children in school are likely to find themselves immediately
separated from their children, and made useless to them, by the
intervention of new educational techniques, technologies,
methods, and languages. School systems innovate as compul-
sively and eagerly as factories. (*What Are People For?* 162-63,
ellipses mine)

The real danger of this is clearly delineated in "Higher Education and
Home Defense," for this system of education produces the kind of people
who attended the agriculture conference in *Remembering*; they are

the purest sort of careerists—"upwardly mobile" transients
who will permit no stay or place to interrupt their personal
advance. They must have no local allegiances; they must not
have a local point of view. In order to be able to desecrate,
endanger, or destroy a *place*, after all, one must be able to leave
it and to forget it. (*Home Economics* 51)

Berry writes to instruct the reader in alternatives to what he considers the
unhealthy ways of the dominant culture. He writes, too, out of a sense of
urgency, not unlike Dante's, in defense of his home and its rural way of life
and against the professionals and careerists who exploit it: "The hegemony
of professionals and professionalism erects itself on local failure, and from
then on the locality exists as a market for consumer goods and as a source
of 'raw material,' human and natural" (*What Are People For?* 164). Even this

recalls the *Commedia*, for Dante also saw his home city being desecrated not only by its political factions, but by mercenaries and outsiders, especially the ecclesiastical authorities operating out of the Vatican in the interest of advancing their own careers and political ambitions. He conceived his *Commedia* in defense of his home, seeing the necessary connection between individual and collective spiritual health and the health of a particular place that people in the fullness of their lives inhabit.

This is yet another reason why the *Commedia*, a poem containing history (in Pound's definition of an epic), is an appropriate model—not only does Dante enter the "great community" himself by conversing with Virgil, but his poem is also about a home place—Florence. As a political exile, Dante's *agon* has its source in the civil strife of a city against itself; he is moved to denounce Florence, but not self-righteously, for, in his identification with the city, he acknowledges his own sinful condition. Over the years of his own tragic separation, Dante remembers the history of his home city, Florence, and by telling the agonizing stories of its actual people, living and dead, struggles to be reconciled to it. Dante, in this sense, fulfills Berry's definition of a "regional" writer, because he writes out of a passionate love and yearning for a place and an equally passionate anger against the injustices committed there against his person, against others, and against the place itself. Berry writes, "Community life . . . is tragic, and it is so because it involves unremittingly the need to survive mortality, partiality, and evil" (*What Are People For?* 77). The writer is nonetheless obligated to tell the stories of a community and remain faithful to, and not abandon, it.

Both the *Commedia* and *Remembering* aim to instruct their readers in the best way of living, spiritually and as good citizens in place. Berry's use of Dante is not the product of a literary self-consciousness or academic allusiveness, but of passionate convictions about the purpose of literature in the common culture (which is only common at the point that it is local):

> For one thing, such a culture contains, and conveys to succeeding generations, the history of the use of the place and the knowledge of how the place may be lived in and used. For another, the pattern of *reminding* (emphasis mine) implies affection for the place and respect for it, and so, finally, the

> local culture will carry the knowledge of how the place may be
> well and lovingly used, and also the implicit command to use
> it only well and lovingly. (*What Are People For?* 166)

For Berry, reminding is re-membering, the renewal of the knowledge that
enables people to live fully and completely as members of a healthy communal and familial order of care and affection for a place. In *Remembering*,
Andy recognizes his sin of separation and overcomes his anger over his
severed member, which can never be healed, in order to heal his psyche
and be reconciled to himself, his family, and Port William. The love that
"moves the sun and the other stars" in the *Commedia* moves Andy in this
direction; this love addresses the issue of *human* ecology, because it is the
means of sustaining the human community. The following visionary moment, one that harks back to the "resplendent glory" of San Francisco earlier in the novel, brings Andy home to the essential nature of this love:

> . . . Andy looks and sees the town and the fields around it, Port
> William and its countryside as he never saw or dreamed them,
> the signs everywhere upon them of the care of a longer love
> than any who have lived there have ever imagined. . . . And in
> the fields and the town, walking, standing, or sitting under the
> trees, resting and talking together in the peace of a sabbath
> profound and bright, are people of such beauty that he weeps
> to see them. He sees that these are the membership of one
> another and of the place . . . in which they live and move.
>
> He sees that they are the dead, and they are alive. He sees
> that he lives in eternity as he lives in time, and nothing is lost.
> (*Remembering* 123, ellipses mine)

These last lines answer the key moment of crisis in the *Commedia*, in
Inferno XXXIV. 25, Dante's supreme moment of spiritual incoherence: "Io
non mori', e non rimassi vivo"—"I did not die and I did not remain alive."
Berry echoes these lines in the context of Andy's spiritual rapture, a
Dantean Paradisal vision in which Andy enters into the "great community"
of all the inhabitants who ever lived in Port William—in Pound's words,
Andy makes it "all cohere once again" (the essential task of epic writing).

This communal coherence also answers Andy's vision of spiritual rupture at the beginning of the novel, the man devouring himself. For both Berry and Dante, Paradise does not represent a transcendence of history so much as a reconciliation, a revelation of its spiritual coherence—we note that Dante, in the *Paradiso*, visits people who were exemplars of spiritual and civic virtue during their time on earth and that he returns abruptly to earth after coming before God in a culminating visionary moment. Thus remembering and returning are for Dante critical aspects of his spiritual revitalization. In the act of remembering and returning, "nothing is lost," which is perhaps the most essential reason why Andy comes back and why Berry writes this novel with Dante in mind; why Berry himself decided, like his father, to return to Port Royal, Kentucky; and why he places a premium on the preservation of cultural memory. Cultural memory, in spiritual, moral and practical terms, reveals the coherence of a place and is the means of sustenance, one that is most profoundly ecological, for, in human culture as in nature, "the known/returns to be known again" (*Collected Poems* 105). Even when organisms die they return to the soil to replenish it and bring forth new life. Thus Berry, punningly (and possibly echoing Whitman as well), compares building a healthy culture to building a healthy soil with composting leaves:

> A human community, too, must collect leaves and stories, and turn them to account. It must build soil, and build that memory of itself—in lore and story and song—that will be its culture. These two kinds of accumulation, of local soil and local culture, are intimately related. (*What Are People For?* 154)

To which Berry adds: "A human community, then, if it is to last long, must exert a sort of centripetal force, holding local soil and local memory in place" (*What Are People For?* 155). A society that is ecologically and culturally healthy is impossible when collective memory no longer serves either to preserve the best practices or to criticize its worst practices. Literature does its part by retaining its most ancient didactic function of remembering. *Remembering*, a marriage of argument and art, serves this function, in the home defense.

WORKS CITED

Berry, Wendell. *Collected Poems.* San Francisco: North Point, 1985.

——. *A Continuous Harmony: Essays Cultural and Agricultural.* New York Harcourt, 1972.

——. *The Hidden Wound.* San Francisco: North Point, 1989.

——. *Home Economics.* San Francisco: North Point, 1987.

——. *Remembering.* San Francisco: North Point, 1988.

——. *Standing by Words.* San Francisco: North Point, 1983.

——. *The Unsettling of America: Culture and Agriculture.* San Francisco: Sierra Club, 1977.

——. *What Are People For?* San Francisco: North Point, 1990.

Jackson, Wes. *Altars of Unhewn Stone: Science and the Earth.* San Francisco: North Point, 1987.

His Dailyness

Donald Hall

Some poets remain intimate with the dailyness of life: Thomas Hardy, Gary Snyder. Some poets in their poems imply a removed and holy place, not daily at all: Dylan Thomas, John Milton, G. M. Hopkins. Each way can belong to a great poet; and a great poet, sometimes, can have it both ways: George Herbert's poems are holy, separate, *and* stitch themselves from the intimate fabric of every day. I love the dailyness of Wendell Berry, his line and image integrated with breathing, breakfast, and the working day—or the unworking Sabbath, for that matter. Glancing through the *Collected Poems*, where I have scrawled grateful swoop-marks beside many poems, I am struck by how many poems speak small notes-of-the-day. Many exemplify Berry's pervasive Kentucky wit:

Throwing Away the Mail

Nothing is simple,
not even simplification.
Thus, throwing away
the mail, I exchange
the complexity of duty
for the simplicity of guilt.

Daily; but note that he begins to define an abstract system, distinctions made not only between duty and guilt but also between complexity and simplicity. There is also his typical exaggeration, by which he exchanges his Japanese kimono (of precise observation) for the costume of a tall tale, description by fantasy:

The First

The first man who whistled
thought he had a wren in his mouth.
He went around all day
with his lips puckered,
afraid to swallow.

Did he notice that "swallow" is another bird? (Sure. Doubtless after he wrote it down.) Then there's the irresistible combination of grief and joy, the idiom of Eden:

A Meeting

In a dream I meet
my dead friend. He has,
I know, gone long and far,
and yet he is the same
for the dead are changeless.
They grow no older.
It is I who have changed,
grown strange to what I was.
Yet I, the changed one,
ask: "How you been?"
He grins and looks at me.
"I been eating peaches
off some mighty fine trees."

The dreamer gains this gift of combination. Or—one more example—there's the ear or mind which remains open for messages from ordinary things.

Falling Asleep

Raindrops on the tin roof.
What do they say?
We have all
Been here before.

If as a poet you wait on language (or vision) to embody the extreme moment. . . . Well, if you are Hopkins we are grateful that you waited. . . . Most of us would surely miss what the daily-poet remains ready for. He or she remains attentive to hear the day's world sing its songs.

Five Notes on the Didactic Tradition, in Praise of Wendell Berry

Lionel Basney

1

In these notes I want to bring together, for celebration, some of Berry's poems and one of the oldest traditions of literary thinking. I do this to make two points: that one of the marks of courage in Berry's poetry is its embodying the excellence of this tradition; and that the tradition may be better understood by being seen in an excellent recent example.

Even this modest project contains a difficulty, however, and this is that the tradition awakened in Berry's poetry has been for some time in a state of complicated disrepute. "Didactic" poetry—and the notion, common in literary thought from Plato to Johnson, that poetry does and should instruct—seem to have no place in romantic thinking, whose assumptions we still accept. Accepting them makes it seem that a didactic poetry would have to be coercive and imaginatively inert—that it would deal in abstractions rather than in live consciousness. That this misrepresents the didactic tradition, I cannot demonstrate in five notes. But the undefended, undefined label, "didactic" (as a hostile term), has been attached to Berry's work, and I may be able to show how badly it fits by showing how Berry has grasped what is essential, and alive, in the actual tradition.

Teachers recur in Berry's fiction and poetry, but they are seldom academics. They are usually older friends, who teach by passing on the practical and emotional wisdom that make up their way of life. One is Owen Flood, in the opening poems of *The Wheel*; the weight, the high spiritual value, of his practical wisdom is plain in Berry's imagining him as a Virgil to Berry's Dante. This vision of teaching lies behind the point Berry often makes in prose, that American education has betrayed its calling by accepting conditions that divorce it from the cultural health it ought to preserve. The calling has been lost in the drive to make teaching a career, to break off academic specialties that can be pursued in narrowly academic ways and rewarded with academic success. What this breaking off means to the culture as a whole is loss of useable understanding.

The connection between wisdom and practical living brings us quickly to the heart of the didactic tradition, and to our difficulty with it. "Didactic" is today a term of automatic disapproval. It claims to identify an aesthetic fault—preachiness, doctrine worn on the sleeve—but the usage feels disingenuous, if not dishonest. It has begged the question traditional didactic critics, Horace, Sidney, or Johnson, put at the center of their understanding of poetry: the question of what art contributes to a people's way of life. For Horace, poetry is *idonea vitae*, helpful to life, because it promotes wisdom; and wisdom is a matter of knowing and performing obligation. Poetry sings the understandings, and undertakings, that make a sustained cultural life possible.

Critics who use "didactic" to condemn are also, implicitly, talking about culture as a whole. Their assumption is that culture has no common understandings or undertakings. This assumption, however, is what begs the question; for it conceals a further, unargued assumption: that the evolution of social practice, wherever it may take us, is self-justifying. This is itself a cultural dogma; it is the one dogma anti-didactic critics will allow art to teach. Which means that their objection to the didactic is, at base, an objection to a certain set of obligations, not to the idea that art brings obligations with it.

To say that Berry's poetry can be didactic, then, means that it envisions a specific wisdom, and also the traditional sense of art and culture that gives art the task of teaching this wisdom. I am not suggesting that Berry set out to exemplify a critical tradition. He came to it, I think, through the concrete understandings and undertakings he found at work on the native hill.

If I had to commit myself to a genetic plot of how this happened I would say: first came the devotion to a place (that is, the natural and human community-in-place Berry was born into); then the perception, avoidable only by deliberate blindness, that this place was in harm's way; then the unfolding, both as definition and as defense, of the traditional values of this place; then the understanding, reaching across American history to its European roots, of what the health of this place would require.

I don't offer this, however, either as a biographical chart or as the only theoretical way art approaches the didactic. But something like this seems to be implied by the growth of Berry's writing. What this series of insights shares with Horace and the others is the conviction that living depends on a frame of order which embraces the smaller orders—natural, practical, social, aesthetic—on which we erect effort and judgment: and that art is answerable for its functioning within this order. Working out from Port Royal, Berry found Horace and the others waiting, so to speak, in the same understanding and with the same undertakings.

2

Poetry teaches by affording a vision of, and by praising, a fruitful, moral, coherent way of life. This is, I think, what Horace means by wisdom, since he associates it not with a creed or a system, but with specific obligations the poet, as a person, owes to other people.

It follows that good didactic poetry is not abstract. Here two distinctions must be made. The first is between an abstraction and a general term. One thing that nourishes our antipathy to the didactic is a confusion of these uses of words. The confusion is not merely semantic. It results as well from conviction that living creates its values as it goes along—so that any general, governing, or traditional term must necessarily be out of touch with concrete living, and therefore abstract. In the didactic tradition this was not so. When cultural conditions were thought to be incarnating principles, general words could have substance, felt weight.

Many of Berry's lyrics turn on general words, ones it would be easy to think of as abstract if they were not placed among particular meanings. Some of these poems announce general terms in their titles, such as "Grace":

> The woods is shining this morning.
> Red, gold and green, the leaves
> lie on the ground, or fall,
> or hang full of light in the air still. . . .
> See how without confusion it is
> all that it is, and how flawless
> its grace is. . . .

Grace as a term of theological explanation is surely abstract; as a felt condition it may be concrete and general at the same time. The woods' grace is both actual beauty and its quality of containing and conferring blessedness. But to use "grace" for these qualities also allows the woods to be a context for understanding the human life going near it. "Grace" does not subsume woods to human life, or vice versa, but names the way common to both.

Often in Berry's poems, however, the general element is not a term but a precept. Here a second distinction must be made, between a precept in a poem and the working of the poem as a whole. From "A Discipline":

> It is the time's discipline to think
> of the death of all living, and yet live.

This is clearly preceptual. It lays an intellectual obligation on us: not to accept the discipline is to deny the reality of "the time." As the concluding couplet, the lines are obviously meant to fix the obligation in our response to the poem, in our gain from it. But the precept has the weight of the rest of the poem behind it because it does not exhaust the poem, which builds up its weight out of other things that precept: irony ("Turn toward the holocaust"), image, symbol ("a blazing cocoon"), variety of tone, intensity and lightness ("the kiss of a pretty girl").

It may be Berry's use of explicit precept that bothers readers who complain of his didacticism. The precept expects more of us than appreciation. We are required to agree or disagree, to grant the obligation or reject it. But the adoption need not be simple or mechanical. The irony of the poem's first line, "Turn toward the holocaust," bitter as it is, is not a simple irony: the line is not covertly saying, "turn away from it." Rather it recommends an adoption which must itself be complex—confronting the fact, taking the pressure of it, feeling an adequate rejection that grows out of knowledge. The complexity of the opening sentence sets the condition for the concluding precept.

3

Didactic poetry teaches through many voices and forms. Of course the tradition provided for a poetry of precept. Once the three-part division of styles began to be standard, it was assumed that, as the high style went with epic and tragedy, and the low with comedy, the middle went with the calm voice of civic instruction. Johnson analyzed Pope's *Essays* in the confidence that setting out systematic belief was one of the things poetry did. (It was one of the things romantic poetry didn't do—with the result that principle had to enter poetry disguised, for instance, as lyric effusion: "Ring out the feud of rich and poor, / Ring in redress to all mankind"). But if didactic verse sets out a concrete, complicated vision of life, there is no reason why many tones of voice, and therefore many genres, cannot speak of this vision and how it is, or is not, put into practice.

One of the odd things about criticism of Berry's poetry has been the charge that he writes only one kind of verse, that of "high sayings." In fact (setting aside "Uncle Rad Milton and the Pup," which Berry sometimes introduces as an epic), one encounters elegy, satire, lyric, narrative, song (and hymn), epigram. And there are inventions: the "history" poems in *Clearing*, and the longer short-lined lyrics that are not primarily personal in reference (some of the "Window Poems," and others such as "The River Bridged and Forgot").

An issue Berry returns to often in his prose is decorum—fitting means to ends in an adequately complex sense of context. The issue bridges the space between writing and other crafts. Answering questions of decorum, we are evaluating the scale, mood, style, and personal bias of our means. Decorum also raises the question of generic difference within disciplines— kinds of poetry appropriate to different themes and occasions, kinds of carpentry fitted to different forms of comfort. The vision of a complete culture that animates didactic writing implies a whole range of work—in writing, a marshalling of genres and tones of voice.

It also implies allying poetry (or allying it again) with other verbal forms that have the same purpose—in Berry's case, with prayer, with "sayings," with songs and hymns, with "discipline" (or catechism), with oration and sermon. The genre I want to comment on, however, at a little more length, is satire. What didactic intention does for satire is to save it from being an exercise of distaste; it gives ridicule the substance of stated principle and values. What satire does for the didactic impulse is to sharpen it and focus it on immediate conditions; and satire's irony keeps this focusing from the flatness of simple denunciation: the irony, for instance, in—

> Love the quick profit, the annual raise,
> vacation with pay. Want more
> of everything ready-made. Be afraid
> to know your neighbors and to die.

This is a simpler, more direct, more topical irony than "Turn toward the holocaust." It recommends what it in fact condemns. But the poem does not remain in this vein. Its irony becomes more complicated when the orders the poem is issuing are, in fact, to be obeyed:

> Love the Lord.
> Love the world. Work for nothing.
> Take all that you have and be poor.
> Love someone who does not deserve it.

There is still a satiric edge here; irony is still alive—first, because of the internal tensions of the sentences (possess and be poor); second, because the poem echoes Biblical injunctions we are all familiar with, but don't expect to hear from the mouth of the mad farmer (or from madness at all); third, because, despite our familiarity with these injunctions, we know that no one obeys them (or that to obey them would be a scandal), and so to repeat them "seriously" is ironic, and the more serious the saying the greater the irony.

The example is from "Manifesto: The Mad Farmer Liberation Front," one of Berry's most widely known poems. Satiric irony was not the only thing the mad farmer could do. He stood so far off from ordinary society that he could preach without hampering respectability. (He could even preach to a text, as in "The Mad Farmer Manifesto: The First Amendment," text by Jefferson.) The self-consciousness of the farmer's waywardness let Berry urge one vision while registering respect for others—

It is not the only or the easiest
way to come to the truth. It is one way.

—that is, to resolve one of the difficulties of didactic writing in a time of diversity.

The mad farmer is Berry's one extended experiment in the half-dramatized persona. Generally, Berry in his poems has spoken for himself—however partial, canny, and sidelong this speaking may have been in relation to the man himself—and this changes the problem of generic difference slightly, to one of the ranges of tone available to a single voice. This limitation is not enjoined on the writer by didactic intention; but I think it is encouraged. One of the pleasures we seek in this kind of writing is the pleasure of being talked to seriously (not always gravely) by an interesting, flexible, responsible voice we recognize both in its eloquence and in its games. The voice is not proof of its vision. It is a pledge of faithfulness to the vision.

4

Didactic poetry bears witness to a community of minds and voices. This is one of the dividing lines between the romantic poem and its predecessors: the romantic poem, the evidence and enactment of individual consciousness, must free itself from other voices. Didactic writing does not require that the individual voice merge itself with all others; we have just noted the value of a recognizable voice. But it is required—or will tend, inevitably—to affirm its community with other voices which have spoken the same wisdom.

There are two communities here, distinct but reconcilable. The first is the immediate community the poet serves by singing the wisdom it needs. This, for Berry, is the community-in-place-and-time known variously as Port Royal, Port William, and "here." Berry's poetry records the facts of this place and time, records its speech—"'That social life don't get / down the row, does it, boy?'"—and watches its people—

> By the fall of years I know how it has been
> With Jack Beechum, Mat Feltner, Elton Penn

—all fictional characters, of course, but with prototypes in actual people like Owen Flood. The poetry also draws on the community: it is the example, the test, the evidence of the poem's vision. The exemplary community has to be seen to be believed.

The other community of the didactic voice is the community of past and distant voices which have spoken the same wisdom, defining one tradition. This community differs in kind from the other: binding across time and place, immanent in many situations but recognizably persisting. Berry's work—and again this is probably typical of didactic writing—has come to reveal how the two communities overlap: or, perhaps, how the first is a student of the second.

Another way of saying this is that Berry has looked for ways of revealing how the wisdom of the second, transhistorical community has been implicit in the wisdom of Port William all along. The power to say this has grown, less through growth of insight than through technical invention. In *Openings* and *Farming: A Hand Book*, the most insistently visible community is the one which war and cultural degradation are destroying; while hope and health seem to be embodied in the individual in the fields. I don't think Berry ever believed this to be true. The apparent restriction of the vision was partly the result of a poetic mode, the brief personal lyric, put to a large social function. Undoubtedly the form dramatized powerful feeling. The prophetic ambition packed into these lyrics gave the best of them ("To Think of the Life of a Man") an extraordinary gravity. But the form also allowed for the misapprehension of Berry's vision as "isolated farmer against the world"—the belief, as David Perkins said in his *History of Modern Poetry*, Volume 2, that truth is what happens on twelve acres of Kentucky farmland.

Of course Berry asserts this, in a sense: what is true "here" must be true elsewhere: greed here is greed there, and so are the contrasting virtues. But the heroic (or mad/heroic) figure of the farmer shaking his fist at the warplanes is now less important. (Not because the farmer has left his fields, nor because the warplanes are no longer flying.) Other things implicit in the earlier work have become plainer, more powerful: the frank use of traditional language, specifically Scripture; the use of imagery generalized by long association with given belief. Other forms have been invented, which allow for a less individual, more communal singing: the long medita-tive lyrics of *Clearing* and after, the elegies of *The Wheel*, and its dance-songs (with their evocation of "my people"), and the hymns of *Sabbaths*.

> All that passes descends,
> and ascends again unseen
> into the light . . .
> And every gift is perfect
> in its beginning, for it
> is "from above and cometh down
> from the Father of lights."
> Gravity is grace.

In *Farming*, the light and the dark—life and death, knowledge and mystery, the human world and the chthonic world, air and soil—turn in the poems in an almost incantatory way. Sanford Budick remarks that in Dryden, images of light stand somewhere between literal and figurative, and this is how they work in Berry's poetry as well. But here the Scriptural quotation makes explicit what was implicit all along, that to see the light in Port William as both physical and spiritual is to accept the vision of a very long and authoritative spiritual tradition. The vision is not being imported or imposed: Port William was Christian all along. It is being put forward, now, as the admitted source of power, the traditional representation of the numen: "O light come down to earth, be praised!"

5

My last note is not *about* didactic poetry, but about a note *of* it, as catholi-city was once a note *of* the church. One note not often struck in recent poetry is dignity. We hear gravity, or perhaps a kind of gray sobriety, which is the tonality of endless self-specification. Dignity comes of not being yourself alone. (This is true even of the tragic isolates: they are great because their suffering seems to be the suffering humanity has always endured.) The rhetorical danger of trying for dignity is obvious: strutting and bellowing, as Hamlet said. The danger is nearer in a day of colloquial style. But making the lyric voice draw on the resources of traditional voices reintroduces the possibility.

Many technical things could be said of how dignity is accomplished in Berry's verse. Some have already been mentioned here, in other contexts, such as the use of general terms and the quotation of Scripture. Another is the use of unfolding parallelism:

> Though I am silent
> there is singing around me.
> Though I am dark
> there is vision around me.
> Though I am heavy
> there is flight around me.

Another is a consciously emphatic syntax, half-formal, half-colloquial: "Not again in this flesh will I see / the old trees stand here. . . ." But technique does not account for the persistent dignity of this poetry. It is the formal but not the final cause. Dignity becomes possible the moment the poem is made the instrument of a validity larger than itself. Dignity is the presence of a more generous order.

The courage of most poetry these days is risk, chance, idiosyncrasy, isolation, campaign: running as fast as you can. It is a desperate courage, because it does not know what it serves. The courage of a didactic poetry is different: it is faithfulness, eloquence, measure, completeness: standing still. These are the forms of courage you encounter in Berry's work. I say this to make it clear that my notes are a celebration of what he has done. Having taken the most serious account of our cultural perplexities in his essays, having imagined an exemplary community in his fiction, he has found the sources of eloquent poetry in the vision of an ultimately spiritual wholeness. And the foundation of this vision has been the tradition of wisdom he has set his poems to sing.

Tangible Mystery
in the Poetry
of Wendell Berry

William C. Johnson

Wendell Berry's writing affirms the intimate partnership between earth and spirit, a bond whose roots are at once biblical—"The earth is full of the goodness of the Lord" (Psalm 33)—and practical, since Berry writes out of, and back to, his long experience of working a Kentucky farm. He is sensitive to the world's body, the deep reserves of meaning growing from the earth into the human mind, heart, and community. His poetry enjoins mystery through a ritual of loving observation, in which work and play are part of the earth and its (human and non-human) creatures. The meaning of ritual can be felt and understood as living energy informed and bounded by sacred mystery.

The bond between creature and place is sacred. Earth gives life; tradition teaches habits of responsibility for life. But as Berry has reminded us, "the great disaster of human history" has been "the conceptual division between the holy and the world" (*A Continuous Harmony* 6), so that, in turn, "the history of our time has been to a considerable extent a movement of the center of consciousness away from home" (*The Unsettling of America* 53).

Berry's poetry offers a counter-challenge to this disembodied "intelligence." In testifying to the indwelling presence of the sacred in land, creature, and community, Berry offers us an ecology centered in spirit.

We sense this spirit in an early poem, "The Sycamore":

> It is a fact, sublime, mystical and unassailable.
> In all the country there is no other like it.
> I recognize in it a principle, an indwelling
> the same as itself, and greater, that I would be ruled by.
> I see that it stands in its place, and feeds upon it,
> and is fed upon, and is native, and maker. (*Collected Poems* 65)

The sycamore embodies a polarity of fact and presence. "An indwelling /
the same as itself, and greater" articulates the interpenetration of flesh and
energy in a tangible, yet mysterious way. What dwells within all living
things is at once concrete and mystical, the self and the self's ruler. As it
feeds in its place, and in turn is fed upon, the tree is "native, and maker." In
Berry, the biblical idea of losing the self to find it, extends to all creation:
". . . moved / by what moves / all else, you move" (*Collected Poems* 145).

To be ruled in this way is to enter the life of the other, to be keenly
aware of its intricate subtlety, to respect its nature as other, as we see in
another early poem, "The Snake":

> At the end of October
> I found on the floor of the woods
> a small snake whose back
> was patterned with the dark
> of the dead leaves he lay on.
> His body was thickened with a mouse
> or small bird. He was cold,
> so stuporous with his full belly
> and the fall air that he hardly
> troubled to flicker his tongue.
> I held him a long time, thinking
> of the perfection of the dark
> marking on his back, the death

> that swelled in him, his living cold.
> Now the cold of him stays
> in my hand, and I think of him
> lying below the frost,
> big with death to nourish him
> during a long sleep. (*Collected Poems* 58)

The poem locates the snake in its native place. The speaker's reverence is clear, but does not overcome or replace our sense of the snake's presence: "I held him a long time, thinking. . . ." Language is the mental "niche" through which we enter the snake's life. "The perfection of the dark" completes this life. The snake is part of its place, and part of the food-chain enters the snake, dying to warm it. The phrase "his living cold" plays on the mingling of death-in-life, for the snake embodies cold in three senses: it is cold-blooded; it is warmed by what has died and become cold; and the memory of its cold, in the poet's hand, kindles his thought. If every biology is a counter-physics, then Berry's ecology is ultimately, though never exclusively, meta-physics. We will all one day enter the "long sleep" of death, as food for something else, but in this at least our lives will not have been wasted. We live, breathe, and die in partnership.

In its domestic and natural reference, Berry's diction is simple, but never simplistic. His words reflect a direct encounter with place, thing, and creature. His line is supple, but not consciously rhetorical; his syntax graceful, at times almost biblical, but austere in its adherence to "necessary things" (*Collected Poems* 128). He has the directness and immediacy of Williams, the historical perspicacity of Pound, the colloquial freshness of Frost. But the deeper "sources" of his work are not literary. They are rooted firmly in land, family, and community, in the mysterious, transactional relations in and through which we dwell. One inevitably thinks of Berry-like images to describe this: raking, haying, birthing, scattering seed. But the meaning of such acts transcends sociology or soil-chemistry. The will to live responsibly hinges on an ever-deepening relation between earth and spirit, often expressed in a language of dwelling. In some of Berry's best poems, this quality of dwelling becomes mysteriously accessible. He has a gift for bringing what is unseen into knowable, if never containable, presence, as in "To the Unseeable Animal":

Being, whose flesh dissolves
at our glance, knower
of the secret sums and measures,
you are always here,
dwelling in the oldest sycamores,
visiting the faithful springs
when they are dark and the foxes
have crept to their edges.
I have come upon pools
in streams, places overgrown
with the woods' shadow,
where I knew you had rested,
watching the little fish
hang still in the flow;
as I approached they seemed
particles of your clear mind
disappearing among the rocks.
I have waked deep in the woods
in the early morning, sure
that while I slept
your gaze passed over me.
That we do not know you
is your perfection
and our hope. The darkness
keeps us near you. (*Collected Poems* 140-1)

The "Being" the poem addresses is at once generic—generative of all beings—and specific. "Flesh dissolves" into a presence, not a thing, but is felt nonetheless as something near. Spirit in Berry's poems is never abstract, but present in the tacit pre-dispositions of sense, the interior, unseen energies of place and creature. The poem makes it clear why Berry's diction remains aptly general rather than strictly visual. He avoids what Coleridge called "the despotism of the eye" through an attentiveness to inner form, the felt life, the "clear mind" of other beings, their places. For an instant, we see through the unseen animal's eyes, as it watches the fishes suspended in the current like "particles," not of our own abstraction (the atom), but of the co-mingling of beast and stream, the "clear mind." The language is not sharply visual, but deeply visionary.

In his timeless conservatism, Berry is radical. In an uncivilized time, he writes of subjects as old as civilization itself, keeping early traditions alive not merely by writing *about* them, but by learning *from* them, through the active life of work and the contemplative enjoyment of its fruits. Not surprisingly, one of his favorite images is the seed, as in these lines from "The Man Born to Farming":

> What miraculous seed has he swallowed
> that the unending sentence of his love flows out of his mouth
> like a vine clinging in the sunlight, and like water
> descending in the dark? (*Collected Poems* 103)

The "sentence" of the farmer's love is labor, its literal and figurative fruits. Unless words grow from authentic labor with the earth, transforming what Thoreau called this "cubic foot of flesh" (for flesh is sustained, Antaeus-like, by the earth), no seed will sprout. Clear expression springs not from rational concept, but from subtle purpose:

> . . . the seed doesn't swell
> in its husk by reason, but loves
> itself, obeys light which is its
> own thought and argues the leaf in secret. (*Collected Poems* 32)

The seed is the germ of inborn mystery—a crisp, bonelike ovum we can hold in our hand. It is a microcosm of creation itself, enacting the original unity as it unfolds: tendril, cotyledon, stem, leaf, fruit. Its growth enjoins earth and light in plant-form (homologically as root and blossom) as it enters the intricate alchemy of temperature, moisture, and soil, the metamorphoses that articulate our mystery. For we too are seeds, each with our chance to root:

> But our memory of ourselves, hard earned
> is one of the land's seeds, as a seed
> is the memory of the life of its kind in its place,

> to pass on into life the knowledge
> of what has died. (*Collected Poems* 159)

And memory lives in the marriage of people to the earth and to each other. Indeed, Berry offers a vision of marriage as the central ritual within biological and human communities, something we must undertake out of a respect for mystery. The spouse is the "way" and the "place," marriage a journey into and by means of mystery, a mutual quest for the country of marriage:

> You are the known way leading always to the unknown,
> and you are the known place to which the unknown is always
> leading me back. (*Collected Poems* 147)

Mystery is not the absurdity of a chance universe, but the ineffable, living presence-in-commitment opening outward into family, household, nature, and cosmos—back to the divine name. Fear, uncertainty, and the inevitability of death bring us back to refuge and renewal in bonds of love and work, bonds increasingly tenuous in a society that severs not only male and female, but work and home. To be so divided "reduces our largeness, our mystery, to a petty and sickly comprehensibility" (*Home Economics* 141). Berry reminds men and women alike that gender is but the biological expression of Being itself, both natural and spiritual, and as such must not be used as a weapon or an enticement, but humbly respected as a powerful manifestation of life itself, human, natural, and metaphysical.

Berry's poems do not often appear in popular, academic anthologies. His pastoralism, his traditional diction, the absence of psychologism, all bespeak a poetic mode currently unpopular. Berry is suspect because he is not, in the conventional sense of the term, a humanist poet. He does not explore the freedom of the isolate human self. In Berry's poems, humanity finds and expresses meaning not through a life apart, but as "a part." The numinous resides not in the cloying confines of ego or in the shortcircuitings of failed relationships, but in the intricate web of creation itself, experienced from a finite, local perspective. We discover freedom through responsible action for the whole, as but one form of being in the scale of creation. Hence the profound significance of restraint, both formal and conceptual, in Berry's work—his deeply felt, and deeply intelligent, response to the necessary limits of a life in its place.

Berry's imagination, then, is *embodied*, expressed through local intelligence and practice. Unlike many of his contemporaries, he does not break out of experience to "language itself," the infinitely regressive complexities of disembodied meaning: since the idea of language for itself, severed from the living world, would violate the web of creation. To write (or read) in this way, is tantamount to studying animals in a zoo, or farming by computer. Berry's language springs from, and back to, experience in the body of the earth household, the ancient "body politic." He reminds us that poetic as well as biological form exercises restraint, to preserve its own integrity and that of others, to respond adequately and responsibly to its superior subject, life—which in Berry is ultimately though never exclusively spiritual. Any meanings are possible, but only certain meanings are responsible, hence finally meaningful. Through his attunement to what is greater than human, Berry offers us healing. Hearing his voice, we enter the dance of creation, joining hands with unknown partners in a ring circling past and future:

> When you meet, and hold love
> in your arms, regardless of all,
> the unknown will dance away from you
> toward the horizon of light.
> Our names will flutter
> on these hills like little fires. (*Collected Poems* 264)

WORKS CITED

Berry, Wendell. *Collected Poems*. San Francisco: North Point Press, 1985.
————. *A Continuous Harmony*. New York: Harcourt, 1972.
————. *Home Economics*. San Francisco: North Point Press, 1987.
————. *The Unsettling of America*. New York: Sierra Club & Avon, 1977.

Farm as Form:
Wendell Berry's Sabbaths

Jeffery Alan Triggs

Rhyme and meter have certainly known their ups and downs in this century. Early on, it seemed that the great modernist poets, Eliot, Pound, Williams, and Stevens, had more or less banished them from serious poetry in favor of free verse. Of course, there was the recalcitrant figure of Frost, who refused to play his tennis without a net; and even Eliot, whose verse was soaked in Elizabethan cadences, warned that "good" *vers libre* was not really *libre* at all, that the ghost of a meter lurked somewhere behind the arras. Still, the main effort seemed to be, as Pound remarked of Williams's practice, to break the back of the pentameter line. Then the 'thirties ushered in what seemed to be a new dispensation altogether on the authority, practical as well as theoretical, of the New Critics. Perhaps someone had noticed that Eliot's favorite poets, the Elizabethans, had used rhyme and meter even in witty and paradoxical poems of undissociated sensibility. In any event, poet-critics like Ransom, Tate, Winters, and Blackmur not only heaped critical praise on unified, formally structured lyrics, but wrote such poetry themselves: lyric units making use of rhyme and meter as integral parts of their meaning. A glance at the magazine verse of the 'forties and 'fifties reveals that in spite of the continuing presence of the older modernists (as well as such isolated followers as Oppen and Zukofsky), the short, rhyming lyric was very much the mainstream poem in America.

The 'sixties brought an end to all this. Actually, the signs of change were in the air a decade earlier: the rediscovery of Ezra Pound, the emergence of the Black Mountain School and the Beat poets, the critical enthusiasm that began to devalue Donne's ratiocinative irony in favor of the passionate mysticism of the later Blake. But in the 'sixties, in America at least, the lid blew off traditional form altogether. Even punctuation was "out." Established poets like Lowell and Berryman, who had matured under the aegis of Ransom, made influential leaps into free verse. And a whole generation of younger poets, schooled at least in the precepts of the New Critics as disseminated in the ubiquitous text, *Understanding Poetry*, echoed Robert Bly's battle cry against "the Tate-Ransom nostalgia for jails" ("Looking for Dragon Smoke").

Wendell Berry is part of this generation, and for most of his career he has followed its predilections as to form. It is of some present interest, therefore, that in his most recent book of poems, *Sabbaths*, he has made a major investment in traditional forms. It is worth considering just what Berry expects to get from formal verse that he could not have gotten from his earlier, free verse forms. Could this be simply a nostalgia for the poetry of his student days, the poetic equivalent of the recent revival of "Greek" life on college campuses, or does it suggest something new and necessary in his expression?

Like most poets of his generation, Berry had worked away from his origins in the new critical school toward the establishment of a personal poetic idiom. Along with Bly and many others in the 'sixties, he sampled the promiscuous freedom of surreal techniques and felt the attraction of political protest poetry. Unlike Bly, however, Berry did not consider such impulses sufficient in themselves, either philosophically or poetically. Instead, he sought to reflect and articulate in his poetry the vital rhythms and satisfactions of rural life, and more specifically the life of a farmer at home in his community and accepting of his place in nature, what he has called "a system of nested systems" (*Standing by Words* 46). Berry's model of the nurturing (as opposed to the exploiting) man has been the farmer "whose life does not travel / along any road, toward / any other place, / but is a journey back and forth / in rows," (*Collected Poems* 242). The idiom of poems like this one from *The Wheel* (1982), a supple, short-lined free verse, was admirably equipped to express Berry's mystical but rooted sense of farming. The language is simple and concrete—it is on easy, conversational terms with the outside world—but free enough, in telling moments, to rise into the higher temperatures of mystical expression. Its natural speech rhythms trace the landscape of hilly farmland and woods in Berry's native Kentucky, accurately registering the encroachments of one upon the other, reading closely the history of the land.

There has long been, perhaps, a latent contradiction in Berry's work between the formality of his philosophical positions, the "system of systems," for instance, which he calls "an updated, ecological version of the Great Chain of Being" (*Standing by Words* 46-7), and the colloquial freedom of his chosen verse forms. In his critical writings, Berry has been aware of a correlation between natural and literary form. In his essay, "Standing by Words," he notes that "one of the great practical uses of literary disciplines . . . is to resist glibness—to slow language down and make it thoughtful. This accounts for the influence of verse, in its formal aspect, within the dynamics of the growth of language: verse checks the merely impulsive flow of speech, subjects it to another pulse, to measure, to extra-linguistic considerations; by inducing the hesitations of difficulty, it admits into language the influence of the Muse and of musing" (*Standing by Words* 28). For Berry, a "merely impulsive flow of speech" is the linguistic correlative of philosophical rootlessness, of not knowing one's place in the decorum of nature. Such rootlessness represents a licentious and therefore dangerous freedom in a world whose survival is dependent on maintaining the delicate balance of its constituents. In another essay, "Poetry and Place," Berry relates the organic form of community and place to literary form: "one's farm . . . is indeed a form. It's not a literary form, but it is *like* a literary form. . . . Like any other form, it requires us to do some things, and forbids us to do others. Some acts are fitting and becoming, and some acts are not. If we fail to do what is required and if we do what is forbidden, we exclude ourselves from the mercy of Nature" (*Standing by Words* 192-3).

The somewhat prescriptive, neo-Augustan tone of much of this (the reader will note Berry's eighteenth century-like capitalization of Nature) is not surprising in a critic who has just spent a number of pages defending Alexander Pope's attitude toward nature against some rather ill-considered criticism by Robert Bly. But it may seem surprising coming from a poet who for most of his career has practiced a form of free verse. Berry has always been one for consistency, however, and in *Standing by Words* he is bringing his critical thinking into line with certain philosophical attitudes puzzled out over the last twenty years. It is fitting that the author of *The Unsettling of America* should come to see that "the work of poetic form is coherence, joining things that need to be joined, as marriage joins them—in words by which a man or a woman can stand, words confirmable in acts . . . . Thus, for a couple, marriage is an entrance into a timeless community. So, for a poet (or a reader), is the mastery of poetic form. Joining the form, we join all that the form has joined" (*Standing by Words* 213). Berry does not luxuriate in currently fashionable notions of the indeterminacy of meaning. For him, form is not merely abstract or arbitrary, but is the animating structure of life as it is really lived in all variety. It stands as warp to the weft of raw and transient experience.

In *Sabbaths*, the poet in Berry is attempting to work out the practical implications of these ideas, and it represents a daring move. It is always dangerous (though perhaps also necessary) for an artist to leave behind modes of expression he has found both congenial and serviceable. Therefore, on a certain level, the technique of *Sabbaths* is less assured than that of *The Wheel*. There is a "Sunday Best" tone in certain of these poems, a self-conscious formality that issues in biblical allusions and formal allusions to poets like George Herbert and Dante (a couple of the poems make use of *terza rima*). Occasionally, there are lapses into hollow versifying, as in these lines:

> To sit and look at light-filled leaves
> May let us see, or seem to see,
> Far backward as through clearer eyes
> To what unsighted hope believes:
> The blessed conviviality
> That sang Creation's seventh sunrise . . . (*Sabbaths* 9)

At moments like this, one has the impression that the meter and rhyme scheme are controlling Berry rather than the other way around. The nature mysticism here seems schoolish and awkward compared to such supple free verse efforts as "On the Hill Late at Night" (*Farming: A Hand Book*, 1970):

> The ripe grassheads bend in the starlight
> in the soft wind, beneath them the darkness
> of the grass, fathomless, the long blades
> rising out of the well of time. Cars
> travel the valley roads below me, their lights
> finding the dark, and racing on. Above
> their roar is a silence I have suddenly heard,
> and felt the country turn under the stars
> toward dawn. (*Collected Poems* 113)

Here the free verse rhythm delicately mimes the movement of "the soft wind," while the harsh caesura before "Cars," staring into the blank space at the end of the line, suggests the intrusion of the modern world. Equally effective is the other delayed caesura before "Above," whose hushed, lifting quality ushers in the tone of revelation in the next lines. The point is not to make invidious comparisons, but to demonstrate something of the masterly free verse technique Berry has risked leaving behind.

A good part of *Sabbaths*, on the other hand, does attain to mastery of a different kind. One might consider these lines from the poem beginning "Here where the dark-sourced stream brims up":

> From cloud to sea to cloud, I climb
> The deer road through the leafless trees
> Under a wind that batters limb
> On limb, still roaring as it has
>
> Two nights and days, cold in slow spring.
> But ancient song in a wild throat
>
> Recalls itself and starts to sing
> In storm-cleared light; and the bloodroot,

> Twinleaf, and rue anemone
> Among bare shadows rise, keep faith
> With what they have been and will be
> Again: frail stem and leaf, mere breath
>
> Of white and starry bloom, each form
> Recalling itself to its place
> And time. (44-5)

Here Berry's native poetic instincts are fully in command of the form, wrestling with it (notice the sharp but telling enjambments) and rendering it supple enough to express his sense of the spring's explosive renewal. The language is concrete and colloquial, but the ultimate confines of the form nicely suggest the order of nature itself, which contains the explosion.

This order, together with the accommodations we must make with it as living beings within nature, is one of the main themes of *Sabbaths*, as it has become perhaps the central theme in all of Berry's varied work. The notion of nature as embodying a strict form of polyphonous spontaneity finds expression in a number of poems. Keenly and delicately, Berry observes its outlines:

> Over the river in loud flood,
> in the wind deep and broad
> under the unending sky, pair
> by pair, the swallows again,
> with tender exactitude,
> play out their line
> in arcs laid on the air,
> as soon as made, not there. (*Sabbaths* 71)

The effort of all these prepositional phrases is to place the flight of the swallows, evanescent at once and enduring, in the larger form of nature, and the method, the form is to match the swallows' own "tender exactitude." (Indeed, Berry's use of prepositions throughout his work to establish a firm sense of place would repay critical study.) When Berry wishes to place our "intellect so ravenous to know," it is with *terza rima* stanzas, invoking the authority of Dante and his ordered sense of the life of the world and man's position in it. Human intellect, as Berry has often told us and tells us once again, "must finally know the dark" (*Sabbaths* 35). Recognizing that "all orders made by mortal hand or love / Or thought come to a margin of their kind, / Are lost in an order we are ignorant of," we must learn to

> Leave word and argument, be dark and still,
> And come into the joy of healing shade.
> Rest from your work. Be still and dark until
>
> You grow as unopposing, unafraid
> As the young trees, without thought or belief;
> Until the shadow Sabbath light has made
>
> Shudders, breaks open, shines in every leaf. (36)

Not only here, but throughout *Sabbaths* this mystical play of light and dark on the leaves extends a prominent metaphorical concern of Berry's earlier work.

This poem touches also on two related issues of Berry's present book: his structuring of the work around various "Sabbaths" marked off by years from 1979 to 1986, and his repeated use of overtly Christian references. This latter has been an issue of some contention. Berry has never been a writer to fit anyone's preconceptions. Critics have chided him on occasion both for "preachiness" and lack of religious orthodoxy. I have argued on other occasions ("Moving the Dark to Wholeness" and "A Kinship of the Fields") that Berry is a deeply religious poet, though his religion has never been that of the strictly orthodox Christian, encompassing as it does the myths of eastern religions (the "Wheel of Life") and the Winnebago Indians as easily as the stories of the Bible. Berry is suspicious of the tendency in certain strains of orthodox Christianity to exalt spirit at the expense of the body, which he considers ultimately corruptive of man's respect for nature. And he prefers the cyclical notion of time held typically by "primitive" religions to the linear vision of time enshrined in Christian dogma. On the other hand, in *Standing by Words* he explicitly accepts a sphere of religious interest standing protectively above and outside the system of systems:

> There has to be a religious interest of some kind above the ecogenetic [i.e., "the interest of the whole 'household' in which life is lived" (48)]. . . . the system of systems is enclosed within mystery, in which some truth can be known, but never all truth. . . . you cannot speak or act in your own best interest without espousing and serving a higher interest. It is not knowledge that enforces this realization, but the humbling awareness of the insufficiency of knowledge, of mystery. (49-50)

This is not, as some critics have charged, an attempt to make a religion of ecology, for Berry insists that the religious sphere, the sphere of ultimate mystery, stands outside the ecological system, but it is vague enough in its contours to disquiet the churchly. Even in *Sabbaths*, the "mad farmer" in Berry maintains his wonted "contrariness":

> The bell calls in the town . . . .
> I hear, but understand
> Contrarily, and walk into the woods. (*Sabbaths* 10)

What is new in *Sabbaths* is not a conversion to orthodox theology, but the acceptance of a traditional, Christian vocabulary, which enforces a certain measure or form on Berry's previously unsponsored religious expression. The book is sprinkled with references to Resurrection, Creation, Paradise, Heaven, Eden, the forfeit Garden, the Lord, the Maker, God and His sepulcher, and of course Sabbath, all with their appropriate, numinous capitalizations. Berry makes discrete use, however, of this formal nomenclature. Resurrection, for instance, is not limited in its connotations to a doctrine of Christian theology, but serves to illuminate through its formal control the vast and spontaneous energy of spring:

> The tracked rut
> Fills and levels; here nothing grieves

In the risen season. Past life
Lives in the living. Resurrection
Is in the way each maple leaf
Commemorates its kind, by connection

Outreaching understanding. (*Sabbaths* 7)

The resurrection here is unique to Berry's sense of religious interest, of mystery "outreaching understanding." It functions to denominate formally the vital return of the year. Berry absorbs the Christian nomenclature in all its intricacy, as he does the devices of formal verse, in order to express his own sense of the delicate relations informing the system of systems and the religious mystery surrounding it.

The title of the book itself is redolent with specifically Judeo-Christian associations. The word "sabbath" has its origins in a Hebrew verb meaning "to rest," and is used in the Bible to indicate the seventh day of the Creation, the Lord's day of rest. It has come to suggest either the seventh or the first day of the week, and in Christian tradition it is synonymous with Sunday, a day of abstinence from work and the day of Jesus' Resurrection. All these senses are allowed play in Berry's work, which gives it an uncommon associative density. For Berry, the sabbath represents the formal closure of one of the chief cycles of time. It marks at once the end of the work week and the beginning of the new week. Its repeatability in difference makes it especially important to a poet like Berry, who has long been interested in cyclical time as manifested in days, in the seasons, and in generations. The cyclical structure of *Sabbaths* is reinforced by its subdivision into eight parts, which refer specifically to eight years and by implication to eight days in the closed circle of a week, from Sunday to Sunday. Thus the sabbath connects meaningfully with the symbolism of the *Wheel of Life* and Berry's earlier work.

The epigraph of *Sabbaths* is taken from Isaiah 14:7: "The whole earth is at rest, and is quiet: they break forth into singing." This is an uncharacteristically gentle passage amidst a series of oracles of the Lord's doom on the *hubris* of foreign peoples, in the case of Chapter 14, the Babylonians. The eighth verse continues: "Yea, the fir trees rejoice at thee [the King of Babylon], and the cedars of Lebanon, saying, Since thou art laid down, no feller is come up against us." The "singing" would appear to be of the trees, and metonymically of the birds in the trees. That such singing should come as the harbinger of a great empire's destruction sets Berry's work subtly in a darker key. The absent fellers of trees are by implication modern Americans as well as Babylonians, with relevant environmental overtones. This suggests, of course, one of Berry's central themes, exploiting man's possibly imminent destruction of nature. The new note is the implication of divine, retributive force, and Berry's own awe in the face of it:

> He steps
> Amid a foliage of song
> No tone of which has passed his lips.
> Watching, silent, he shifts among
>
> The shiftings of the day, himself
> A shifting of the day's design
> Whose outline is in doubt, unsafe,
> And dark. One time, less learned in pain,
>
> He thought the earth was firm, his own,
> But now he knows that all not raised
> By fire, by water is brought down. (*Sabbaths* 73)

The song of the trees and "the day's design" take on a dark and fearfully numinous aspect for one "learned in pain." Berry has always cautioned us to prepare for disaster by accepting death as a necessary part of nature, but here he seems conscious of the ultimately mysterious causes in the religious sphere. *Sabbaths*, however, represents also a provisionally hopeful dissipation of Berry's fears through meditative attention to nature and its intricate balance:

> what is afraid of me comes
> and lives a while in my sight.
> What it fears in me leaves me,
> and the fear of me leaves it.
> It sings, and I hear its song.

Then what I am afraid of comes.
I live for a while in its sight.
What I fear in it leaves it,
and the fear of it leaves me.
It sings, and I hear its song.

After days of labor,
mute in my consternations,
I hear my song at last,
and I sing it. As we sing
the day turns, the trees move. (*Sabbaths* 5-6)

The day of rest after labor becomes for Berry the day of unburdening his fears, of dispersing consternations in a formal song echoing the formality of nature itself.

The emphasis on the sabbath as a day of rest, however, contrasts with the workday feeling of so many of Berry's earlier farm poems. Where the farm poems allow mystical intuitions to arise from everyday encounters with the ecological sphere of nature, the sabbath poems, though rooted in nature, seek actively to penetrate the religious sphere through formal meditation, the prescribed activity of the seventh day. This occasions a greater reliance on mystical tropes than is usual in Berry's work, particularly in the pervasive images of light and song:

Thrush song, stream song, holy love
That flows through earthly forms and folds,
The song of Heaven's Sabbath fleshed
In throat and ear, in stream and stone,
A grace living here as we live,
Move my mind now to that which holds
Things as they change. (*Sabbaths* 47)

The "songs" here function on several interactive levels of metaphor: the simple and familiar comparison of a bird's sounds with song, the somewhat less familiar comparison of the sound of the stream with song, the parataxis identifying these with the notion of "holy love," and the mystical representation of "the song of heaven's Sabbath," which involves them all, and amounts to an experience of grace. Berry's meditative scheme also issues in a more elaborate and rhetorically driven syntax:

> Not again in this flesh will I see
> the old trees stand here as they did,
> weighty creatures made of light, delight
> of their making straight in them and well,
> whatever blight our blindness was or made,
> however thought or act might fail. (*Sabbaths* 81)

The extravagance of Berry's diction is held beautifully in check by the sinuous grammatical structure. Through formal artifice, Berry achieves, on this occasion and on many others in *Sabbaths*, a fine linguistic balance, an order cognate with those of agriculture and nature.

Berry's technique in *Sabbaths*, far from being simply nostalgic, an empty exercise in the "well-made" poetry of the 'forties and 'fifties, represents a logical and compelling development of his craft. Berry has long been a poet of the internal relations—instinctual, formal, and ritual—which join together families, communities, even the past and future generations with themselves, with the ecological system, and with the ultimate sphere of mystery. For Berry, the farm is one, though not the only, form which embodies and sustains these relations:

> Enclosing the field within bounds
> sets it apart from the boundless
> of which it was, and is, a part,
> and places it within care.
> The bounds of the field bind
> the mind to it. A bride
> adorned, the field now wears
> the green veil of a season's
> abounding. Open the gate!
> Open it wide, that time
> and hunger may come in. (*Sabbaths* 18)

This poem, whose immediate subject is the farm as form, a dominant idea in Berry's work, might serve also as an *ars poetica* for *Sabbaths*. Artistic form shares the responsibilities of all other vital forms: recognizing limits and orders, and joining things to create new and fertile orders. Thus may time and hunger, the uncontrollables, be domesticated to substantial pleasures.

WORKS CITED

Berry, Wendell. *Collected Poems 1957-1982.* San Francisco: North Point Press, 1985.
——— . *Sabbaths.* San Francisco: North Point Press, 1987.
——— . *Standing by Words.* San Francisco: North Point Press, 1983.
Bly, Robert. "Looking for Dragon Smoke." *Naked Poetry: Recent American Poetry in Open Forms.* Ed. Stephen Berg and Robert Mezey. Indianapolis and New York: The Bobbs-Merrill Company, Inc., 1969: 161-4.
Triggs, Jeffery Alan. "A Kinship of the Fields: Farming in the Poetry of R. S. Thomas and Wendell Berry." *North Dakota Quarterly* 57.2 (Spring 1989): 92-102.
——— . "Moving the Dark to Wholeness: The Elegies of Wendell Berry." *The Literary Review* 31.3 (Spring 1988): 279-92.

Wendell Berry:
Selected Bibliography

Paul Merchant

WORKS BY WENDELL BERRY:
FICTION:

Nathan Coulter Houghton Mifflin 1960; revised text, North Point 1985 (cloth and paper).

Reviews:

Lamott, Kenneth. *San Francisco Chronicle* 29 May 1960, 22.

Fraser, C. Gerald. *New York Times Book Review* 90 (30 June 1985), 32.

Snyder, Ross. *Christian Century* 77 (5 October 1960), 1156.

A Place on Earth Harcourt Brace 1967; revised text, North Point 1985 (cloth and paper).

Reviews:

Davenport, Guy. *National Review* 19 (14 November 1967), 1282.

Mitchell, Henry. *New York Times Book Review* 72 (15 October 1987), 54.

Perrin, Noel. *New York Times Book Review* 88 (18 December 1983), 8, 16.

Pritchard, William H. *Hudson Review* 21 (Summer 1968), 368-9.

Stegner, Page. *Southern Review* 5 (Winter 1969), 275-7.

Sterne, R. C. *Nation* 206 (1 April 1968), 448.

The Memory of Old Jack Harcourt Brace Janovich 1974; Harbrace 1975, Harvest Books 1986 (paper).

Reviews:

Cheuse, Alan. *Nation* 219 (28 September 1974), 278.

Ditsky, John M. *University of Windsor Review* Fall/Winter 1974, 112.

Frakes, James R. *New York Times Book Review* 31 March 1974, 38.

Hall, Joan Joffe. *New Republic* 170 (6 April 1974), 26-7.

Marcus, Griel. *Rolling Stone* 4 December 1975, 89.

Yardley, Jonathan. *Washington Post Book World* 3 March 1974, 3.

————. *Sewanee Review* 82 (July 1974), 542-3.

Spacks, Patricia Meyer. *Hudson Review* 27 (Summer 1974), 288-92.

The Wild Birds: Six Stories of the Port William Membership North Point 1986 (cloth), 1989 (paper).

Contains: Thicker Than Liquor / Where Did They Go? / It Wasn't Me / The Boundary / That Distant Land / The Wild Birds.

Reviews:

Basney, Lionel. *Christianity and Literature* 37.3 (Spring 1988), 54-5.

Morris, Gregory L. *Prairie Schooner* 60.4 (Winter 1986), 102-4.

Mosher, Howard Frank. *New York Times Book Review* 91 (13 April 1986), 22.

Parini, Jay. *Times Literary Supplement* 26 June 1987, 698.

Polsgrove, Carol. *Nation* 242.17 (3 May 1986), 626-7.

Swann, Brian. *Commonweal* 113 (6 June 1986), 345.

unsigned, *Los Angeles Times Book Review* 27 April 1986, 6.

Remembering North Point 1988 (cloth), 1990 (paper).

Reviews:

Ewald, Richard. *American Book Review* 11 (September/October 1989), 21.

Johnson, Greg. *New York Times Book Review* 94 (1 January 1989), 14.

Karlins, Mark. *Parabola* 14 (May 1989), 112-6.

Kilgo, James. *Sewanee Review* 97 (April 1989), lvi-ii.

Little, Charles E. *Wilderness* 52 (Summer 1989), 59.

McEntyre, John. *Christian Century* 106 (15 February 1989), 182-3.

unsigned, *Progressive* 52 (December 1988), 46-7.

unsigned, *Washington Post Book World* 18 (11 December 1988), 8.

POETRY:

November twenty six, nineteen sixty three George Braziller 1964 (with illustrations by Ben Shahn).

The Broken Ground Harcourt Brace 1964; Jonathan Cape, London 1966.
   Reviews:
   Carruth, Hayden. *Poetry* 106 (July 1965), 309-11.
   Crossley-Holland, Kevin. *Books and Bookmen* 12 (December 1966), 58.
   Davis, D. M. *National Observer* 4 (4 January 1965), 17.
   Dickey, William. *Hudson Review* 17 (Winter 1964/65), 587-9.
   Fike, Francis K. *Epoch* 14 (Spring 1965), 378-80.
   Gelpi, Albert J. *Southern Review* 3 (Autumn 1967), 1028-9.
   Hazel, Robert. *Kenyon Review* 27 (Spring 1965), 378-80.
   Martz, Louis. *Yale Review* 54 (Summer 1965), 605.
   Pack, Robert. *New York Times Book Review* 70 (17 January 1965), 32.
   unsigned, *Times Literary Supplement* 15 December 1966, 1172.
Openings Harcourt Brace 1968; Harvest Books 1980 (paper).
   Reviews:
   Cooper, Jane. *New York Times Book Review* 22 December 1968, 10.
   Dickey, William. *Hudson Review* 22 (Summer 1969), 362.
   Moran, Ronald. *Southern Review* 8 (Winter 1972), 249-50.
   Stafford, William. *Poetry* 113 (March 1969), 421-2.
   Walsh, Chad. *Washington Post Book World* 3 November 1968, 20.
Findings Prairie Press 1969.
   Review:
   Shaw, Robert B. *Poetry* 117 (November 1970), 108-114.
Farming: A Hand Book Harcourt Brace Jovanovich 1970; Harvest Books
   1971, Harvest/HBJ Books 1986 (paper).
   Reviews:
   Callaghan, Patrick. *Prarie Schooner* 45.3 (Fall 1971), 273-4.
   French, Roberts W. *Nation* 211 (9 November 1970), 472-3.
   Irwin, J. T. *Southern Review* 9 (Summer 1973), 731-2.
   Pritchard, William H. *Poetry* 119 (1971), 159.
The Country of Marriage Harcourt Brace Jovanovich 1973; Harvest Books
   1975, Harvest/HBJ Books 1986 (paper).
   Reviews:
   Allen, Dick. *Poetry* 124 (May 1974), 106-9.
   Robinson, James K. *Southern Review* 11 (July 1975), 671-2.
   unsigned, *Washington Post Book World* 7 (11 February 1973), 95.
An Eastward Look Sand Dollar Press 1974.

Falling Asleep Cold Mountain Press Postcard Series II 1974.

Horses Larkspur Press 1975.

To What Listens Best Cellar Press 1975.

Sayings and Doings Gnomon Press 1975.

> *Review:*
>
> Richardson, D. E. *Southern Review* 12 (October 1976), 879-90.

The Kentucky River: Two Poems Larkspur Press 1976.

There Is Singing Around Me Cold Mountain Press 1976.

Three Memorial Poems Sand Dollar Press 1977.

> *Review:*
>
> Kramer, Lawrence. *Parnassus* 6 (Spring/Summer 1978), 108-12.

Clearing Harcourt Brace Jovanovich 1977; Harvest Books 1977 (paper).

> *Reviews:*
>
> Cotter, James Finn. *America* 137 (20 August 1977), 81-2.
>
> Hall, Donald. *New York Times Book Review* 25 September 1977, 24-6.
>
> Hamburger, Michael. *The Boston University Journal* 25.3 (1978), 69-72.
>
> Ignatow, David. *Partisan Review* 44.2 (Spring 1977), 317.
>
> Kramer, Lawrence. *Parnassus* 6 (Spring/Summer 1978), 108-12.
>
> Parini, Jay. *Virginia Quarterly Review* 54 (Autumn 1978), 762-5.
>
> Stitt, Peter. *Georgia Review* 31.4 (Winter 1977), 955-7.
>
> Young, Vernon. *Hudson Review* 30.4 (Winter 1977-8), 579-81.

The Gift of Gravity The Deerfield Press, Massachusetts/The Gallery Press, Dublin 1979.

A Part North Point 1980 (cloth and paper).

> *Reviews:*
>
> Ditsky, John M. *University of Windsor Review* Fall/Winter 1981, 134.
>
> Hamburger, Michael. *Times Literary Supplement* 10 April 1981, 416.
>
> Lea, S. *Parnassus* 9 (Fall 1981), 131.
>
> Murray, G. E. *Hudson Review* 34 (Spring 1981), 157-8.
>
> Simmons, Tom. *Christian Science Monitor* 73 (30 September 1981), 15.
>
> unsigned, *American Book Review* 3 (July 1981), 6.
>
> unsigned, *Washington Post Book World* 11 (15 February 1981), 8.

The Nativity The Penmaen Press 1981.

> Modern version of a poem by William Dunbar.

The Wheel North Point 1982 (cloth and paper).

Reviews:

Holthaus, Gary H. *Western American Literature* 19.4 (1985), 311-4.

Kinzie, M. *American Poetry Review* 12 (January 1983), 289.

McDowell, Robert. *Hudson Review* 37 (Spring 1984), 129.

Perrin, Noel. *New York Times Book Review* 88 (18 December 1983), 8, 16.

Prunty, Wyatt. *Southern Review* 20.4 (Autumn 1984), 958-60.

unsigned, *Washington Post Book World* 13 (13 March 1983), 10.

Collected Poems 1957-1982 North Point 1985 (cloth), 1987 (paper).

Reviews:

Basney, Lionel. *Christianity and Literature* 35.4 (Summer 1986), 31-2.

———. *The Other Side* 22.5 (June 1986), 56.

Kusma, Greg. *Northwest Review* 25, 111.

McDowell, Robert. *Hudson Review* 38.4 (Winter 1986), 681-2.

Ray, David. *New York Times Book Review* 24 November 1985, 28-9.

Smith, Dave. *Poetry* 147.1 (October 1985), 40-2.

Stitt, Peter. *Georgia Review* 39 (Fall 1985), 635.

Swann, Brian. *Commonweal* 113 (6 June 1986), 345-6.

unsigned, *San Francisco Review of Books* 9 (May 1985), 40.

Some Differences Confluence Press 1987 (cloth and paper).

Sabbaths North Point 1987 (cloth and paper).

Reviews:

Conarroe, Joel. *Commonweal* 114 (4 December 1987), 712.

Cotter, James Finn. *Hudson Review* 41 (Spring 1988), 229-31.

Hosmer, Robert. *America* 158 (7 May 1988), 490.

Shaw, Robert B. *Poetry* 152 (April 1988), 37.

unsigned, *Los Angeles Times Book Review* 8 November 1987, 5.

Traveling at Home Press Alley (limited ed.) 1988; North Point 1989.

Contains: fifteen poems from *Collected Poems 1957-1982* and *Sabbaths* / an excerpt from "A Native Hill" (*The Long-Legged House; Recollected Essays 1965-1980*).

NON-FICTION:

The Rise University of Kentucky, Graves Press 1968.

The Long-Legged House Harcourt Brace Jovanovich 1969; Ballantine 1971 (paper).

Contains: The Tyranny of Charity / The Landscaping of Hell / Strip-Mine Morality in East Kentucky (with postscript, July 1968: A Land Set Aside) / The Nature Consumers / The Loss of the Future / A Statement against the War in Vietnam / Some Thoughts on Citizenship and Conscience in Honor of Don Pratt / The Rise / The Long-Legged House / A Native Hill.

Reviews:

Cadle, Dean. *Southwest Review* 54 (Fall 1969), 436-43.

Johnson, Josephine W. *Nation* 208 (2 June 1969), 707.

Sawyer, Roland. *Christian Science Monitor* 61 (17 June 1969), 9.

The Hidden Wound Houghton Mifflin 1970; Ballantine 1971 (paper); North Point 1989 (paper).

Reviews:

Alexander, Margaret Walker. *Black Scholar* 12 (March 1981), 92

Callaghan, Patrick. *Prairie Schooner.* 45.3 (Fall 1971), 273-4.

Hattman, John W. *Best Sellers* 30.17 (1 December 1970), 374-5.

The Unforeseen Wilderness: an Essay on Kentucky's Red River Gorge with photographs by Eugene Meatyard. University Press of Kentucky 1971. Reprint forthcoming from North Point Press.

A Continuous Harmony; Essays Cultural & Agricultural Harcourt Brace Jovanovich 1972; Harvest Books 1975, Harvest/HBJ Books 1986 (paper).

Contains: A Secular Pilgrimage / Notes from an Absence and a Return / A Homage to Dr. Williams / The Regional Motive / Think Little / Discipline and Hope / In Defense of Literacy / Mayhem in the Industrial Paradise.

Review:

King, Richard H. *New Leader* 56 (19 February 1973), 20-1.

The Unsettling of America: Culture and Agriculture Sierra Club Books, San Francisco 1977; Avon Books 1978, Sierra Club 1986 (paper).

Contains: The Unsettling of America / The Ecological Crisis as a Crisis of Character / The Ecological Crisis as a Crisis of Culture / The Agricultural Crisis as a Crisis of Culture / Living in the Future: The "Modern" Industrial Ideal / The Use of Energy / The Body and the Earth / Jefferson, Morrill, and the Upper Crust / Margins.

Reviews:

Flower, Dean. *Hudson Review* 31 (Spring 1978), 176-7.

Hall, Donald. *New York Times Book Review* 25 September 1977, 24.

Pew, Thomas. *Horticulture* 56 (February 1978), 7-9.

Reiner, Steven. *Atlantic Monthly* 240 (October 1977), 106.

Ruesink, Albert. *Business Horizons* 23 (April 1980), 79-81.

Sanders, Scott. *Progressive* 42 (February 1978), 43.

Weiland, Steven. *Iowa Review* 10.1 (Winter 1979), 99-104.

Young, Thomas Daniel. *Sewanee Review* 86 (Fall 1978), 603-4.

Zito, Tom. *(Manchester) Guardian Weekly* 117 (18 December 1977), 14.

unsigned, *Natural Resources Journal* 18 (July 1978), 693.

unsigned, *Threepenny Review* 6 (Winter 1986), 22.

The Gift of Good Land: Further Essays Cultural and Agricultural North Point 1981 (cloth and paper).

Contains: An Agricultural Journey in Peru / Three Ways of Farming in the Southwest / The Native Grasses and What They Mean / The International Hill Land Symposium / Sanitation and the Small Farm / Horse-Drawn Tools and the Doctrine of Labor Saving / Agricultural Solutions for Agricultural Problems / Energy in Agriculture / Solving for Pattern / The Economics of Subsistence / Family Work / The Reactor and the Garden / A Good Scythe / Looking Ahead / Home of the Free / Going Back—or Ahead—to Horses / A Few Words for Motherhood / A Rescued Farm / An Excellent Homestead / Elmer Lapp's Place / A Talent for Necessity / New Roots for Agricultural Research / Seven Amish Farms / The Gift of Good Land.

Reviews:

Ditsky, John M. *University of Windsor Review* Fall/Winter 1981), 134.

Miller, David S. *Sewanee Review* 92 (January 1984), 160-7.

Pevear, Richard. *Hudson Review* 35.2 (Summer 1982), 341-7.

Swain, R. B. *New York Times Book Review* 86 (20 December 1981), 3.

Woiwode, Larry. *Washington Post Book World* 12 (31 January 1982), 5.

unsigned, *Harper's Magazine* 264 (April 1982), 100.

unsigned, *Village Voice* 26 (23 December 1981), 47.

Recollected Essays 1965-1980 North Point 1981 (cloth and paper).

Contains: from *The Long-Legged House*: The Rise / The Long-Legged

House / A Native Hill; from *The Hidden Wound*: Nick and Aunt Georgie; from *A Continuous Harmony*: Discipline and Hope; from *The Unforeseen Wilderness*: A Country of Edges / An Entrance to the Woods / The Unforeseen Wilderness / The Journey's End; from *The Unsettling of America*: The Body and the Earth; uncollected: The Making of a Marginal Farm.

Reviews:

Coiner, Miles. *Antioch Review* 40 (Spring 1982), 244.

Hudson, Charles. *Georgia Review* 36.1 (Spring 1982), 220-3.

Pevear, Richard. *Hudson Review* 25 (Summer 1982), 341-7.

Scranton, William W. *America* 151 (10 November 1984), 301.

Simonson, H. P. *Western American Literature* 17 (Fall 1982), 263.

Swann, Brian. *Commonweal* 113 (6 June 1986), 345.

Woiwode, Larry. *Washington Post Book World* 12 (31 January 1982), 5.

Standing by Words North Point 1983 (cloth and paper).

Contains: The Specialization of Poetry / Standing by Words / People, Land, and Community / Notes: Specializing Poetry / Poetry and Place / Poetry and Marriage.

Reviews:

Basney, Lionel. *Christianity and Literature* 33.4 (Summer 1984), 70-1.

Davenport, G. *Kenyon Review* 6 (Summer 1984), 108-114.

Matthias, John. *Southern Review* 21 (Winter 1985), 183-203.

Miller, D. S. *Sewanee Review* 92 (Winter 1984), 160.

Parini, Jay. *New England Review/Bread Loaf Quarterly* 6 (Summer 1984), 630.

Perrin, Noel. *New York Times Book Review* 88 (18 December 1983), 8, 16.

Ratiner, Steven. *Christian Science Monitor* 76 (2 March 1984), B4.

Swann, Brian. *Commonweal* 113 (6 June 1986), 345-6.

unsigned, *Los Angeles Times Book Review* 18 December 1983, 7.

Meeting the Expectations of the Land: Essays in Sustainable Agriculture & Stewardship Edited with Wes Jackson and Bruce Colman. North Point 1984.

The Landscape of Harmony: Two Essays on Wildness & Community Introduction by Michael Hamburger. Five Seasons Press, Hereford, England 1987 (paper).

Contains: Preserving Wildness / Does Community Have a Value?

Reviews:

Porritt, Jonathan. *Books for a Change* catalog, London 1987.

Raine, Kathleen. *Resurgence* Winter 1987/88.

Home Economics North Point 1987 (cloth and paper).

Contains: Letter to Wes Jackson / Getting Along with Nature / Irish Journal / Higher Education and Home Defense / Two Economies / The Loss of the University / Property, Patriotism, and National Defense / Men and Women in Search of Common Ground / Six Agricultural Fallacies / A Nation Rich in Natural Resources / Preserving Wildness / A Good Farmer of the Old School / A Defense of the Family Farm / Does Community Have a Value?

Reviews:

Allen, Dick. *Hudson Review* 41 (Summer 1988), 409-15.

Barbarese, J. T. *Georgia Review* 43 (Spring 1989), 208-9.

Franklin, K. E. *Wilderness* 51 (Fall 1987), 62-3.

Hyde, Lewis. *New York Times Book Review* 92 (27 September 1987), 30.

Polsgrove, Carol. *Sierra* 73 (March 1988), 88-90.

Smith, Page. *Christian Science Monitor* 79 (3 July 1987), B1, B8.

What Are People For? North Point 1990 (cloth and paper).

Contains: Damage / Healing / A Remarkable Man / Harry Caudill in the Cumberlands / A Few Words in Favor of Edward Abbey / Wallace Stegner and the Great Community / A Poem of Difficult Hope / Style and Grace / Writer and Region / The Responsibility of the Poet / God and Country / A Practical Harmony / An Argument for Diversity / What Are People For? / Waste / Economy and Pleasure / The Pleasures of Eating / The Work of Local Culture / Why I Am Not Going to Buy a Computer / Feminism, the Body, and the Machine / Word and Flesh / Nature as Measure.

Review:

McKibben, Bill. *New York Review of Books* 14 June 1990, 30-4.

Harlan Hubbard: Life and Work University Press of Kentucky 1990 (forthcoming).

UNCOLLECTED NON-FICTION:

Preface to Masanobu Fukuoka, *The One-Straw Revolution*, Rodale Press 1978, Bantam Books 1985.

"The Art of Living Right," an Interview with Gregory McNamee and
James R. Hepworth, *The Bloomsbury Review* June-August 1983; reprinted
in Gregory McNamee, *Living in Words: Interviews fro* The Bloomsbury
Review *1981-1988*, Breitenbush Books 1988.

Introduction to J. Russell Smith, *Tree Crops*, Island Press Books 1987.

Foreword to Gary Paul Nabhan, *Enduring Seeds*, North Point 1989.

Introduction to T. Stanwell-Fletcher, *Driftwood Valley*, Penguin Nature
Library 1989.

Foreword to David Kline, *Great Possessions: An Amish Farmer's Journal*, North
Point 1990.

"A Question a Day: A Written Conversation with Wendell Berry,"
interview by Mindy Weinreb, in *Our Other Voices*, edited by John Wheatcroft, Bucknell University Press 1991; reprinted in this volume.

COMMENTARY ON WENDELL BERRY AND HIS WORK:

Askins, Justin. "A Necessary Darkness." *Parnassus* 15 (1989), 317-30.

Basney, Lionel. "Wendell Berry: The Grace that Keeps the World."
The Other Side 23.1 (January/February 1987), 46-8.

————."Having Your Meaning at Hand: Work in Snyder and
Berry." in *World, Self, Poem: Essays on Contemporary Poetry from the "Jubilation
of Poets,"* ed. Leonard Trawick (Kent State University Press, forthcoming).

————."Five Notes on the Didactic Tradition, in Praise of
Wendell Berry," First published in this volume.

Bauer, Douglas. "We Saved Our Land." *Today's Health* 52 (October 1974),
30-4.

Carruth, Hayden. "Human Authenticity in the Face of Massive Multiply-
ing Error." *Parnassus* Spring/Summer 1986, 140-3.

————."Essays for Wendell." First published in this volume.

Collins, Robert. "A More Mingled Music: Wendell Berry's Ambivalent
View of Language." *Modern Poetry Studies* 11 (1982), 35-56.

Cornell, Daniel. "'The Country of Marriage': Wendell Berry's Personal
Political Vision." *Southern Literary Journal* 15.3 (1983), 59-70.

Decker, William. "'Practice Resurrection': The Poesis of Wendell Berry."
North Dakota Quarterly 55.4 (Fall 1987), 170-84.

Dietrich, Mary. "Our Commitment to the Land." *Bluegrass Literary Review* 2.1, 39-44.

Ditsky, John M. "Wendell Berry's Homage to the Apple Tree." *Modern Poetry Studies* 2 (1971), 7-15.

Ehrlich, A. W. *"Publishers Weekly* Interviews Wendell Berry." *Publishers Weekly* 212 (5 September 1977), 10-11.

Esbjornson, Carl D. *"Remembering* and Home Defense." First published in this volume.

Feld, Ross. "The Where, How, Who and the What in Wendell Berry's Writing." First published in this volume.

Fields, Kenneth. "The Hunter's Trail: Poems by Wendell Berry." *Iowa Review* 1 (Winter 1970), 90-9.

Hall, Donald. "His Dailyness." First published in this volume.

Hamburger, Michael. "The Writings of Wendell Berry: An Introduction." *The Landscape of Harmony: Two Essays on Wildness and Community* by Wendell Berry. Five Seasons Press, Hereford, England 1987. Reprinted in this volume.

Hass, Robert. "Wendell Berry: Finding the Land." *Modern Poetry Studies* 2 (1971), 16-38.

Heinzelman, Kurt. "Indigenous Art: the Poetry of Wendell Berry." *Cencrastus* 2 (1980), 34-7.

Helge, Per. "En Amerikansk Moralist." *Studiekamraten* (Lund, Sweden) 67.6 (1985), 3-7.

Hicks, Jack. "A Wendell Berry Checklist [to 1978]." *Bulletin of Bibliography and Magazine Notes* 37 (1980), 127-31.

————."Wendell Berry's Husband to the World: *A Place on Earth."American Literature* 51 (May 1979), 238-54. Reprinted in this volume.

Hiers, John T. "Wendell Berry: Love Poet." *University of Mississippi Studies in English* 5 (1984-7), 100-9.

Jackson, Wes. "On Cultural Capacity." First published in this volume.

Johnson, William C. "Tangible Mystery in the Poetry of Wendell Berry." First published in this volume.

Kusma, Greg. "Wendell Berry's Natural Piety." *Pebble* 8 (1972), 1.

Lang, John. "'Close Mystery': Wendell Berry's Poetry of Incarnation." *Renascence* 35.4 (Summer 1983), 258-68.

Manning, Richard. "Wendell Berry and his Fight against the Red River Dam." *Louisville Courier-Journal and Times* 12 May 1975, C1, C3.

McNamee, Gregory. "Wendell Berry and the Politics of Agriculture." First published in this volume.

Morgan, Speer. "Wendell Berry: A Fatal Singing." *Southern Review* 10.4 (Fall 1974), 865-77.

Nibbelink, Herman. "Thoreau and Wendell Berry: Bachelor and Husband of Nature." *South Atlantic Quarterly* 84 (1985), 127-40. Reprinted in this volume.

Payne, Warren, E. "Wendell Berry and the Natural." *Resonance* 1.2 (1969), 5-16.

Reader, Willie. "A Correspondence with Wendell Berry." *Poets in the South* 1 (1977-8), 27-31.

Rodale, Robert. "The Landscape of Poetry." *Organic Gardening and Farming* 23 (April 1976), 46-52.

Shadle, Mark. "Traveling at Home: Wandering and Return in Wendell Berry." First published in this volume.

Snyder, Gary. "Berry Territory." *Axe Handles*, North Point Press 1983. Reprinted in this volume.

Stegner, Wallace. "A Letter to Wendell Berry." First published in this volume.

Tarbet, Donald W. "Contemporary American Pastoral: A Poetic Faith." *English Record* 23 (Winter 1972), 72-83.

Triggs, Jeffery Alan. "Moving the Dark to Wholeness: The Elegies of Wendell Berry." *The Literary Review* 31.3 (Spring 1988), 279-92.

——."A Kinship of the Fields: Farming in the Poetry of R. S. Thomas and Wendell Berry." *North Dakota Quarterly* 57.2 (Spring 1989), 92-102.

——."Farm as Form: Wendell Berry's *Sabbaths*." First published in this volume.

Waage, Frederick O. "Wendell Berry's History." *Contemporary Poetry* 3.3 (1978), 21-46.

Weatherhead, A. Kingsley. "Poetry: The 1930s to the Present." *American Literary Scholarship* 9 (1971), 229-321.

Weinreb, Mindy. "A Question a Day: A Written Conversation with

Wendell Berry." *Our Other Voices*, ed. John Wheatcroft. Bucknell University Press 1991. Reprinted in this volume.

Weissman, Judith. "An Open Letter." First published in this volume.

Williams, Terry Tempest. "A Full Moon in May." First published in this volume.

Woolley, Bryan. "Wendell Berry." *Louisville Courier-Journal and Times* 4 August 1974, 41-4.

DISSERTATIONS:

Collins, Robert Joseph. "A Secular Pilgrimage: Nature, Place and Morality in the Poetry of Wendell Berry." Unpublished doctoral dissertation, Ohio State University 1978 (DA 39, 4935A).

Cornell, Daniel T. "Practicing Resurrection: Wendell Berry's Georgic Poetry, an Ecological Critique of American Culture." Unpublished doctoral dissertation, Washington State University 1985 (DAI Sept. 1986, 47[3]:951A).

Tolliver, Gary Wayne. "Beyond Pastoral: Wendell Berry and a Literature of Commitment." Unpublished doctoral dissertation, Ohio State University 1978 (DA 39, 6767A-8A).

MAJOR BIBLIOGRAPHIC ENTRIES ON WENDELL BERRY:

Contemporary Literary Criticism vol. 4, ed. Carolyn Riley. Detroit: Gale, 1975, 59-60.

———— vol. 6, ed. Riley & Mendelsohn. Detroit: Gale, 1976, 61-2.

———— vol. 8, ed. Bryfonski & Mendelsohn. Detroit: Gale, 1978, 85-6.

———— vol. 27, ed. Jean C. Stine. Detroit: Gale, 1984, 32-40.

———— vol. 46, ed. Marowski & Matuz. Detroit: Gale, 1988, 69-75.

Contemporary Authors volumes 73-76, ed. Frances Carol Locher. Detroit: Gale, 1978, 55.

Breznau, Anne Kelsch *Critical Survey of Poetry*, ed. Frank N. Magill. Englewood Cliffs, 1982, 146-55.

Driskell, Leon V. *Dictionary of Literary Biography* vol. 5, ed. Donald S. Greiner. Detroit: Gale, 1980, 62-66.

Tolliver, Gary *Dictionary of Literary Biography* vol. 6, ed. James A. Kibler. Detroit: Gale, 1980, 9-14.

Contributors

Lionel Basney teaches literature and writing at Calvin College, and lives in the west Michigan countryside with his wife and two daughters. His poems have appeared in *Shenandoah*, *The Harvard Magazine*, and *The Country Journal*, and his essays in *South Atlantic Quarterly*, *Eighteenth-Century Studies* and other journals. An essay on William Cobbett is forthcoming in the *Sewanee Review*.

Hayden Carruth has lived much of his life in the rural northeast. He is currently professor in the Graduate Creative Writing Program at Syracuse University. His twenty-six books, chiefly of poetry, include also a novel, criticism, and two anthologies. His most recent books are his *Selected Poetry* (1986), *Tell Me Again How the White Heron Rises . . .* (1989), and *The Sleeping Beauty* (rev. ed. 1990). He has been an editor at *Poetry*, *Harper's*, and *The Hudson Review*, and received a total of more than a dozen fellowships and major awards for his writing.

Carl D. Esbjornson is Assistant Professor of American Thought and Language at Michigan State University. He has published articles on Robert Duncan, and is engaged in a study of the historical and cultural roots of sustainable agriculture in the United States.

Ross Feld is the author of three novels, including *Only Shorter* and most recently *Shapes Mistaken* (North Point Press). He has also published a book of criticism, *Philip Guston* (Braziller).

Donald Hall's *Old and New Poems* came out in June 1990, collecting work from 1947 through 1990. In 1988 his book-length poem, *The One Day*, won the National Book Critics Circle Award and the *Los Angeles Times* Book Award.

Michael Hamburger, one of Britain's most notable poets and translators, lives in Suffolk. He has taught at a number of universities in England and the United States. His more than sixty published volumes include a pioneering translation of Hölderlin, and translations of Baudelaire, Beethoven's letters, of Brecht, Nelly Sachs, Günter Grass and many others. Among his critical works are *The Truth of Poetry* (1969) and *Testimonies* (1989), which included his essay on Berry. His *Collected Poems* appeared in 1985, and a new *Selected Poems* was published in 1989. He has won many awards, including Bollingen Fellowships and the Levinson Prize.

Jack Hicks is Associate Professor of English and Director of the Creative Writing Program at the University of California, Davis. His books include *Cutting Edges* and *In the Singer's Temple*, studies of contemporary American fiction. He has contributed articles on Gary Snyder, Truman Capote and Peter Mathiessen to recent critical collections, and is at work on a study of recent American literary non-fiction.

Wes Jackson is President of the Land Institute near Salina, Kansas. He taught at universities in Kansas and California before founding the Land Institute in 1976. Among his many publications are the four books *Man and the Environment* (1970), *New Roots for Agriculture* (1980), *Meeting the Expectations of the Land* (1984, edited with Wendell Berry and Bruce Colman), and *Altars of Unhewn Stone* (1987).

A Pacific northwest native, **William Johnson** is a Professor of English at Lewis-Clark State College, Lewiston, Idaho. His poems and criticism have appeared in *Quarterly West, Mother Earth News, Journal of Aesthetics and Art Criticism, Philological Quarterly*, and *Chaucer Review*. His book, *What Thoreau Said: 'Walden' and the Unsayable*, will be published by the University of Idaho Press in 1991. His first volume of poetry, *At the Wilderness Boundary*, is nearing completion.

Gregory McNamee is the author of *The Return of Richard Nixon* (Harbinger House 1990), a collection of literary and political essays, and of *Inconstant History: Poems and Translations* (Broken Moon Press 1990). He is also the co-editor, with James Hepworth, of *Resist Much, Obey Little: Some Notes on Edward Abbey* (Harbinger House 1989), editor of *Living in Words: Interviews from* The Bloomsbury Review, 1981-1988 (Breitenbush Books 1988), and translator of Sophokles's tragedy *Philoktetes* (Copper Canyon Press 1987). McNamee makes his home in Tucson, Arizona.

Paul Merchant has taught at universities in England, Poland, and America, most recently at Wittenberg University, Ohio. He is the author of four books of poetry and two of translations from modern Greek. His latest collection, *Bone from a Stag's Heart*, was a (British) Poetry Book Society Recommendation in 1988.

Herman Nibbelink is a professor of English at the University of Wisconsin Center-Waukesha. In addition to his essay on Thoreau and Berry, he has explored issues of nature and farm life in American literature in the *Arizona Quarterly, North Dakota Quarterly*, and *Orion Nature Quarterly*. His poems have appeared in the *Great River Review, Madison Review, Passages North, Spoon River Quarterly*, and elsewhere.

Mark Shadle is currently a member of the English-Writing Department and Writing Lab Director at Eastern Oregon State College in La Grande, Oregon. The tension for him between "staying put" and world travel has resulted in a number of explorations of homecoming and sense of place, including a study of Ishmael Reed, an essay on African music in *Pacific Moana Quarterly*, and a study of the poetry of Gavin Selerie in *North Dakota Quarterly*.

Gary Snyder lives and writes in the Sierra Nevada of California. Among his books of poetry are *Myths and Texts* (1960), the Pulitzer Prizewinning *Turtle Island* (1974) and *Axe Handles* (1983). His equally influential prose studies of ecology and mythology include *Earth House Hold* (1969), *He Who Hunted Birds in His Father's Village* (1979), *The Real Work* (1980), and *Good Wild Sacred* (1984).

Wallace Stegner has been mentor to a large number of the best American writers through the writing program at Stanford, where he taught from 1945 to 1971. His published books include his prizewinning first novel, *Remembering Laughter* (1937), *The Big Rock Candy Mountain* (1943), *All the Little Live Things* (1967), *Angle of Repose* (1971), for which he won the Pulitzer Prize, *The Spectator Bird* (1976), and *Crossing to Safety* (1987). He is also the author of ten works of non-fiction, and is an acknowledged master of the short story. His *Collected Stories* appeared in 1990.

Jeffery Triggs directs the OED's new North American Reading Program from Morristown, New Jersey, and writes poetry and essays about poetry and film. He is currently preparing a book comparing contemporary British and American poetry.

Mindy Weinreb's interviews with Wendell Berry, Hayden Carruth and Mary Oliver were published in *Our Other Voices* (1991). She teaches English at Bucknell and was for several years the Associate in the Bucknell Seminar for Younger Poets. "Music in the Combat Zone," a collaboration with composer William Duckworth, was performed and recorded at New Music America last fall.

Judith Weissman is Professor of English at Syracuse University. Her publications include essays in *The Georgia Review* and *The Southern Review* and the major study *Half Savage and Hardy and Free! Women and Rural Radicalism in the Nineteenth-Century Novel* (Wesleyan University Press 1987).

Terry Tempest Williams is naturalist-in-residence at the Utah Museum of Natural History. In addition to numerous published essays, her books, the first two of which won major awards, are *The Secret Language of Snow*

(1984), *Pieces of White Shell—a Journey to Navajoland* (1984), *Between Cattails* (1985), *Coyote's Canyon* (1989), and *Refuge* (scheduled for publication by Viking in 1991). Ms. Williams also teaches at the University of Utah, and is a board member of a number of national conservancy councils.

WENDELL BERRY

Designed by Debra Moloshok.
Typeset by Jan Donnelly, O.S.B.
With invaluable assistance from
Judi Lanphier and Tanya Gonzales.
Text type is Baskerville
with neo-Montauk display.
Printed by McNaughton & Gunn
on acid-free paper.